REFLECTIONS ON THE PSALMS

'Absolutely packed with wisdom It is clearly the fruit of very much reflection—or rather of meditation. It is a tolerant book. It is an exciting book, for it suddenly throws light not just upon the psalm under discussion, but upon one's own darkness of spirit, one's own fumbling and grasping in the shadows of prayer or of penitence.' *Trevor Huddleston*

'In its entirely contemporary way, Dr. Lewis's book is full of the delight, the wish to share that delight, which illuminates every line of Augustine's splendid sermons.'

Elizabeth Jennings in THE OBSERVER

'A brilliant book. Here is a touch of magic interpretation which can do more than all the learned commentaries to make the reading of the Psalms an open door into the world of the Kingdom and the glory of the Lord. A book to buy and keep and read and read again.' CHURCH TIMES

'There is no shirking of problems. In dealing with the puzzles, Dr. Lewis writes with all his accustomed force and charm. I know of no book on the Psalms that can compare with this for interest and stimulating helpfulness.'

A. Gregory Murray in THE TABLET

C. S. LEWIS

*Reflections on
the Psalms*

Collins
FOUNT PAPERBACKS

First published in Great Britain 1961
First issued in Fontana Books 1967
Reprinted in Fount Paperbacks December 1977
Nineteenth impression October 1989

© Literat S. A. 1961
Printed and bound in Great Britain by
William Collins Sons & Co. Ltd, Glasgow

CONTENTS

I

INTRODUCTORY

THIS IS not a work of scholarship. I am no Hebraist, no higher critic, no ancient historian, no archaeologist. I write for the unlearned about things in which I am unlearned myself. If an excuse is needed (and perhaps it is) for writing such a book, my excuse would be something like this. It often happens that two schoolboys can solve difficulties in their work for one another better than the master can. When you took the problem to a master, as we all remember, he was very likely to explain what you understood already, to add a great deal of information which you didn't want, and say nothing at all about the thing that was puzzling you. I have watched this from both sides of the net; for when, as a teacher myself, I have tried to answer questions brought me by pupils, I have sometimes, after a minute, seen that expression settle down on their faces which assured me that they were suffering exactly the same frustration which I had suffered from my own teachers. The fellow-pupil can help more than the master because he knows less. The difficulty we want him to explain is one he has recently met. The expert met it so long ago that he has forgotten. He sees the whole subject, by now, in such a different light that he cannot conceive what is really troubling the pupil; he sees a dozen other difficulties which ought to be troubling him but aren't.

In this book, then, I write as one amateur to another, talking about difficulties I have met, or lights I have gained, when reading the Psalms, with the hope that this might at any rate interest, and sometimes even help, other inexpert readers. I am " comparing notes ", not presuming to instruct. It may appear to some that I have used the Psalms merely as pegs on which to hang a series of miscellaneous essays. I do not know that it would have done any harm if I had written the book that way, and I shall have no grievance against anyone who reads it that way. But that is not how it was in fact written. The thoughts it contains are those to which I found myself driven in reading the Psalms; sometimes by my enjoyment of them, sometimes by meeting with what at first I could not enjoy.

The Psalms were written by many poets and at many different dates. Some, I believe, are allowed to go back to the reign of David; I think certain scholars allow that Psalm 18 (of which a slightly different version occurs in 2 *Samuel* 22) might be by David himself. But many are later than the " captivity ", which we should call the deportation to Babylon. In a scholarly work, chronology would be the first thing to settle : in a book of this sort nothing more need, or can, be said about it.

What must be said, however, is that the Psalms are poems, and poems intended to be sung : not doctrinal treatises, nor even sermons. Those who talk of reading the Bible " as literature " sometimes mean, I think, reading it without attending to the main thing it is about; like reading Burke with no interest in politics, or reading the *Aeneid* with no interest in Rome. That seems to me to be nonsense. But there is a saner sense in which the Bible, since it is after all literature, cannot properly be read except as literature; and the different parts of it as the different sorts of literature they are. Most emphatically the Psalms must be read as poems; as lyrics, with all the licences and all the formalities, the hyperboles, the emotional rather than logical connections, which are proper to lyric poetry. They must be read as poems if they are to be understood; no less than French must be read as French or English as English. Otherwise we shall miss what is in them and think we see what is not.

Their chief formal characteristic, the most obvious element of pattern, is fortunately one that survives in translation. Most readers will know that I mean what the scholars call "parallelism"; that is, the practice of saying the same thing twice in different words. A perfect example is "He that dwelleth in heaven shall laugh them to scorn : the Lord shall have them in derision "(2, 4), or again, "He shall make thy righteousness as clear as the light; and thy just dealing as the noon-day" (37, 6). If this is not recognised as pattern, the reader will either find mares' nests (as some of the older preachers did) in his effort to get a different meaning out of each half of the verse or else feel that it is rather silly.

In reality it is a very pure example of what all pattern, and therefore all art, involves. The principle of art has been defined by someone as "the same in the other". Thus in a country dance you take three steps and then three steps again. That is the same. But the first three are to the right and the second three to the left. That is the other. In a building there may be a wing on one side and a wing on the other, but both of the same shape. In music the composer may say ABC, and then abc, and then αβγ. Rhyme consists in putting together two syllables that have the same sound except for their initial consonants, which are other. "Parallelism" is the characteristically Hebrew form of the same in the other, but it occurs in many English poets too : for example, in Marlowe's

> *Cut is the branch that might have grown*
> *full straight*
> *And burned is Apollo's laurel bough,*

or in the childishly simple form used by the *Cherry Tree Carol,*

> *Joseph was an old man and an old man was he.*

Of course the Parallelism is often partially concealed on purpose (as the balances between masses in a picture may be something far subtler than complete symmetry). And of course other and more complex patterns may be worked in across it, as in Psalm 119, or in 107 with its refrain. I mention only what is most obvious, the Parallelism itself. It is (according to one's point of view) either a wonderful piece of luck or a wise provision of God's, that poetry which was to be turned into all languages should have as its chief formal characteristic one that does not disappear (as mere metre does) in translation.

If we have any taste for poetry we shall enjoy this feature of the Psalms. Even those Christians who cannot enjoy it will respect it; for Our Lord, soaked in the poetic tradition of His country, delighted to use it. " For with what judgement ye judge, ye shall be judged; and with what measure ye mete, it shall be measured to you again " (*Matthew* 7, 2). The second half of the verse makes no logical addition; it echoes, with variation, the first, " Ask, and it shall be given you, seek, and ye shall find; knock and it shall be opened unto you " (7, 7). The advice is given in the first phrase, then twice repeated with different images. We may, if we like, see in this an exclusively practical and didactic purpose; by giving to truths which are infinitely worth remembering this rhythmic and incantatory expression, He made them almost impossible to forget. I like to suspect more. It seems to me appropriate, almost inevitable, that when that great Imagination which in the beginning, for Its own delight and for the delight of men and angels and (in their proper mode) of beasts, had invented and formed the whole world of Nature, submitted to express Itself in human speech, that speech should sometimes be poetry. For poetry too is a little incarnation, giving body to what had been before invisible and inaudible.

I think, too, it will do us no harm to remember that, in becoming Man, He bowed His neck beneath the sweet

yoke of a heredity and early environment. Humanly
speaking, He would have learned this style, if from no
one else (but it was all about Him) from His Mother.
"That we should be saved from our enemies and from
the hands of all that hate us; to perform the mercy pro-
mised to our fathers, and to remember his holy coven-
ant." Here is the same parallelism. (And incidentally, is
this the only aspect in which we can say of His human
nature "He was His Mother's own son"? There is a
fierceness, even a touch of Deborah, mixed with the
sweetness in the *Magnificat* to which most painted
Madonnas do little justice; matching the frequent severity of His own sayings. I am sure the private life of the
holy family was, in many senses, " mild " and " gentle ",
but perhaps hardly in the way some hymn writers have
in mind. One may suspect, on proper occasions, a certain
astringency; and all in what people at Jerusalem regarded as a rough north-country dialect.)

I have not attempted of course to " cover the subject "
even on my own amateurish level. I have stressed, and
omitted, as my own interests led me. I say nothing about
the long historical Psalms, partly because they have
meant less to me, and partly because they seem to call for
little comment. I say the least I can about the history of
the Psalms as parts of various " services "; a wide subject, and not for me. And I begin with those characteristics of the Psalter which are at first most repellent.
Other men of my age will know why. Our generation
was brought up to eat everything on the plate; and it
was the sound principle of nursery gastronomy to polish
off the nasty things first and leave the titbits to the end.

I have worked in the main from the translation
which Anglicans find in their Prayer Book; that of
Coverdale. Even of the old translators he is by no
means the most accurate; and of course a sound
modern scholar has more Hebrew in his little finger than
poor Coverdale had in his whole body. But in beauty,
in poetry, he, and St. Jerome, the great Latin translator,

are beyond all whom I know. I have usually checked, and sometimes corrected, his version from that of Dr. Moffatt.

Finally, as will soon be apparent to any reader, this is not what is called an " apologetic " work. I am nowhere trying to convince unbelievers that Christianity is true. I address those who already believe it, or those who are ready, while reading, to " suspend their disbelief ". A man can't be always defending the truth; there must be a time to feed on it.

I have written, too, as a member of the Church of England, but I have avoided controversial questions as much as possible. At one point I had to explain how I differed on a certain matter both from Roman Catholics and from Fundamentalists : I hope I shall not for this forfeit the goodwill or the prayers of either. Nor do I much fear it. In my experience the bitterest opposition comes neither from them nor from any other thorough-going believers, and not often from atheists, but from semi-believers of all complexions. There are some enlightened and progressive old gentlemen of this sort whom no courtesy can propitiate and no modesty disarm. But then I dare say I am a much more annoying person than I know. (Shall we, perhaps, in Purgatory, see our own faces and hear our own voices as they really were?)

II

"JUDGEMENT" IN THE PSALMS

IF THERE is any thought at which a Christian trembles it is the thought of God's "judgement". The "Day" of Judgement is "that day of wrath, that dreadful day". We pray for God to deliver us "in the hour of death and at the day of judgement". Christian art and literature for centuries have depicted its terrors. This note in Christianity certainly goes back to the teaching of Our Lord Himself; especially to the terrible parable of the Sheep and the Goats. This can leave no conscience untouched, for in it the "Goats" are condemned entirely for their sins of omission; as if to make us fairly sure that the heaviest charge against each of us turns not upon the things he has done but on those he never did—perhaps never dreamed of doing.

It was therefore with great surprise that I first noticed how the Psalmists talk about the judgements of God. They talk like this; "O let the nations rejoice and be glad, for thou shalt judge the folk righteously (67, *4*), " Let the field be joyful . . . all the trees of the wood shall rejoice before the Lord, for he cometh, for he cometh to judge the earth " (96, *12, 13*). Judgement is apparently an occasion of universal rejoicing. People ask for it: "Judge me, O Lord my God, according to thy righteousness " (35, *24*).

The reason for this soon becomes very plain. The ancient Jews, like ourselves, think of God's judgement in terms of an earthly court of justice. The difference is that the Christian pictures the case to be tried as a criminal case with himself in the dock; the Jew pictures it as a civil case with himself as the plaintiff. The one hopes for acquittal, or rather for pardon; the other hopes for a resounding triumph with heavy damages. Hence he prays " judge my quarrel ", or " avenge my cause " (35, 23). And though, as I said a minute ago, Our Lord in the parable of the Sheep and the Goats painted the characteristically Christian picture, in another place He is very characteristically Jewish. Notice what He means by " an unjust judge ". By those words most of us would mean someone like Judge Jeffreys or the creatures who sat on the benches of German tribunals during the Nazi *régime* : someone who bullies witnesses and jurymen in order to convict, and then savagely to punish, innocent men. Once again, we are thinking of a criminal trial. We hope we shall never appear in the dock before such a judge. But the Unjust Judge in the parable is quite a different character. There is no danger of appearing in his court against your will : the difficulty is the opposite— to get into it. It is clearly a civil action. The poor woman (*Luke* 18, *1-5*) has had her little strip of land— room for a pigsty or a hen-run—taken away from her by a richer and more powerful neighbour (nowadays it would be Town-Planners or some other " Body "). And she knows she has a perfectly watertight case. If once she could get it into court and have it tried by the laws of the land, she would be bound to get that strip back. But no one will listen to her, she can't get it tried. No wonder she is anxious for " judgement ".

Behind this lies an age-old and almost world-wide experience which we have been spared. In most places and times it has been very difficult for the " small man " to get his case heard. The judge (and, doubtless, one or two of his underlings) has to be bribed. If you can't afford to " oil his palm " your case will never reach court. Our judges do not receive bribes. (We probably take this blessing too much for granted; it will not remain with us automatically.) We need not therefore be surprised if the Psalms, and the Prophets, are full of the longing for judgement, and regard the announcement that " judgement " is coming as good news. Hundreds and thousands of people who have been stripped of all they possess and who have the right entirely on their side will at last be heard. Of course they are not afraid of judgement. They know their case is unanswerable—if only it could be heard. When God comes to judge, at last it will.

Dozens of passages make the point clear. In Psalm 9 we are told that God will "minister true judgement" (*8*), and that is because He "forgetteth not the complaint of the poor" (*12*). He "defendeth the cause" (that is, the "case") " of the widows" (68, 5). The good king in Psalm 72, 2, will "judge" the people rightly; that is, he will "defend the poor". When God "arises to judgement" he will "help all the meek upon earth" (76, 9), all the timid, helpless people whose wrongs have never been righted yet. When God accuses earthly judges of "wrong judgement", He follows it up by telling them to see that the poor "have right" (82, *2*, *3*).

The "just" judge, then, is primarily he who rights a wrong in a civil case. He would, no doubt, also try a criminal case justly, but that is hardly ever what the Psalmists are thinking of. Christians cry to God for mercy instead of justice; *they* cried to God for justice instead of injustice. The Divine Judge is the defender, the rescuer. Scholars tell me that in the *Book of Judges* the word we so translate might almost be rendered "champions"; for though these "judges" do sometimes perform what we should call judicial functions many of them are much more concerned with rescuing the oppressed Israelites from Philistines and others by force of arms. They are more like Jack the Giant Killer than like a modern judge in a wig. The knights in romances of chivalry who go about rescuing distressed damsels and widows from giants and other tyrants are acting almost as "judges" in the old Hebrew sense : so is the modern solicitor (and I have known such) who does unpaid work for poor clients to save them from wrong.

I think there are very good reasons for regarding the

Christian picture of God's judgement as far more profound and far safer for our souls than the Jewish. But
this does not mean that the Jewish conception must
simply be thrown away. I, at least, believe I can still get
a good deal of nourishment out of it.

It supplements the Christian picture in one important
way. For what alarms us in the Christian picture is the
infinite purity of the standard against which our actions
will be judged. But then we know that none of us will
ever come up to that standard. We are all in the same
boat. We must all pin our hopes on the mercy of God
and the work of Christ, not on our own goodness. Now
the Jewish picture of a civil action sharply reminds us
that perhaps we are faulty not only by the Divine standard (that is a matter of course) but also by a very human
standard which all reasonable people admit and which
we ourselves usually wish to enforce upon others. Almost
certainly there are unsatisfied claims, human claims,
against each one of us. For who can really believe that
in all his dealings with employers and employees, with
husband or wife, with parents and children, in quarrels
and in collaborations, he has always attained (let alone
charity or generosity) mere honesty and fairness? Of
course we forget most of the injuries we have done. But
the injured parties do not forget even if they forgive.
And God does not forget. And even what we can remember is formidable enough. Few of us have always,
in full measure, given our pupils or patients or clients (or
whatever our particular "consumers" may be called)
what we were being paid for. We have not always done
quite our fair share of some tiresome work if we found a
colleague or partner who could be beguiled into carrying
the heavy end.

Our quarrels provide a very good example of the
way in which the Christian and Jewish conceptions
differ, while yet both should be kept in mind. As Christians we must of course repent of all the anger, malice,
and self-will which allowed the discussion to become, on

our side, a quarrel at all. But there is also the question
on a far lower level : " granted the quarrel (we'll go into
that later) did you fight fair?" Or did we not quite
unknowingly falsify the whole issue? Did we pretend to
be angry about one thing when we knew, or could have
known, that our anger had a different and much less pre-
sentable cause? Did we pretend to be " hurt " in our
sensitive and tender feelings (fine natures like ours are so
vulnerable) when envy, ungratified vanity, or thwarted
self-will was our real trouble? Such tactics often succeed.
The other parties give in. They give in not because they
don't know what is really wrong with us but because
they have long known it only too well, and that sleeping
dog can be roused, that skeleton brought out of its cup-
board, only at the cost of imperilling their whole relation-
ship with us. It needs surgery which they know we will
never face. And so we win; by cheating. But the unfair-
ness is very deeply felt. Indeed what is commonly called
" sensitiveness " is the most powerful engine of domestic
tyranny, sometimes a lifelong tyranny. How we should
deal with it in others I am not sure; but we should be
merciless to its first appearances in ourselves.

The constant protests in the Psalms against those who
oppress " the poor " might seem at first to have less application to our own society than to most. But perhaps
this is superficial; perhaps what changes is not the op-
pression but only the identity of " the poor ". It often
happens that someone in my acquaintance gets a demand
from the Income Tax people which he queries. As a result it sometimes comes back to him reduced by anything
up to fifty per cent. One man whom I knew, a solicitor,
went round to the office and asked what they had meant
by the original demand. The creature behind the counter
tittered and said, " Well, there's never any harm in trying
it on." Now when the cheat is thus attempted against
men of the world who know how to look after themselves, no great harm is done. Some time has been
wasted, and we all in some measure share the disgrace of

belonging to a community where such practices are tolerated, but that is all. When, however, that kind of publican sends a similarly dishonest demand to a poor widow, already half starving on a highly taxable "unearned" income (actually earned by years of self-denial on her husband's part) which inflation has reduced to almost nothing, a very different result probably follows. She cannot afford legal help; she understands nothing; she is terrified, and pays—cutting down on the meals and the fuel which were already wholly insufficient. The publican who has successfully "tried it on" with her is precisely "the ungodly" who "for his own lust doth persecute the poor" (10, 2). To be sure, he does this, not like the ancient publican, for his own immediate rakeoff; only to advance himself in the service or to please his masters. This makes a difference. How important that difference is in the eyes of Him who avenges the fatherless and the widow I do not know. The publican may consider the question in the hour of death and will learn the answer at the day of "judgement". (But—who knows?—I may be doing the publicans an injustice. Perhaps they regard their work as a sport and observe game laws; and as other sportsmen will not shoot a sitting bird, so they may reserve their illegal demands for those who can defend themselves and hit back, and would never dream of "trying it on" with the helpless. If so, I can only apologise for my error. If what I have said is unjustified as a rebuke of what they are, it may still be useful as a warning of what they may yet become. Falsehood is habit-forming.)

It will be noticed, however, that I make the Jewish conception of a civil judgement available for my Christian profit by picturing myself as the defendant, not the plaintiff. The writers of the Psalms do not do this. They look forward to "judgement" because they think they have been wronged and hope to see their wrongs righted. There are, indeed, some passages in which the Psalmists approach to Christian humility and wisely lose their self-confidence. Thus in Psalm 50 (one of the finest) God is the accuser (*6-21*); and in 143, *2*, we have the words which most Christians often repeat—" Enter not into judgement with Thy servant, for in Thy sight shall no man living be justified." But these are exceptional. Nearly always the Psalmist is the indignant plaintiff.

He is quite sure, apparently, that his own hands are clean. He never did to others the horrid things that others are doing to him. " If I have done any such thing "—if I ever behaved like so-and-so, then let so-and-so " tread my life down upon the earth " (7, *3-5*). But of course I haven't. It is not as if my enemies are paying me out for any ill turn I ever did them. On the contrary, they have " rewarded me evil for good ". Even after that, I went on exercising the utmost charity towards them. When they were ill I prayed and fasted on their behalf (35, *12-14*).

All this of course has its spiritual danger. It leads into that typically Jewish prison of self-righteousness which Our Lord so often terribly rebuked. We shall have to consider that presently. For the moment, however, I think it is important to make a distinction : between the conviction that one is in the right and the conviction that one is " righteous " is a good man. Since none of us is righteous, the second conviction is always a delusion. But any of us may be, probably all of us at one time or another are, in the right about some particular issue. What is more, the worse man may be in the right against the better man. Their general characters have nothing to do with it. The question whether the disputed pencil belongs to Tommy or Charles is quite distinct from the question which is the nicer little boy, and the parents who allowed the one to influence their decision about the other would be very unfair. (It would be still worse if they said Tommy ought to let Charles have the pencil whether it belonged to him or not, because this would show he had a nice disposition. That may be true, but it is an untimely truth. An exhortation to charity should

not come as rider to a refusal of justice. It is likely to
give Tommy a lifelong conviction that charity is a
sanctimonious dodge for condoning theft and white-
washing favouritism.) We need therefore by no means
assume that the Psalmists are deceived or lying when
they assert that, as against their particular enemies at
some particular moment, they are completely in the
right. Their voices while they say so may grate harshly
on our ear and suggest to us that they are unamiable
people. But that is another matter. And to be wronged
does not commonly make people amiable.

But of course the fatal confusion between being in the
right and being righteous soon falls upon them. In 7,
from which I have already quoted, we see the transition.
In verses 3 to 5 the poet is merely in the right; by verse 8
he is saying " give sentence with me, O Lord, according
to my righteousness and according to the innocency that
is in me ". There is also in many of the Psalms a still
more fatal confusion—that between the desire for justice
and the desire for revenge. These important topics will
have to be treated separately. The self-righteous Psalms
can be dealt with only at a much later stage; the vindictive Psalms, the cursings, we may turn to at once. It is
these that have made the Psalter largely a closed book to
many modern church-goers. Vicars, not unnaturally, are
afraid to set before their congregations poems so full of
that passion to which Our Lord's teaching allows no
quarter. Yet there must be some Christian use to be
made of them; if, at least, we still believe (as I do) that
all Holy Scripture is in some sense—though not all parts
of it in the same sense—the word of God. (The sense in
which I understand this will be explained later.)

THE CURSINGS

IN SOME of the Psalms the spirit of hatred which strikes us in the face is like the heat from a furnace mouth. In others the same spirit ceases to be frightful only by becoming (to a modern mind) almost comic in it naïvety.

Examples of the first can be found all over the Psalter, but perhaps the worst is in 109. The poet prays that an ungodly man may rule over his enemy and that " Satan " may stand at his right hand (5). This probably does not mean what a Christian reader naturally supposes. The " Satan " is an accuser, perhaps an informer. When the enemy is tried, let him be convicted and sentenced, " and let his prayer be turned into sin " (6). This again means, I think, not his prayers to God, but his supplications to a human judge, which are to make things all the hotter for him (double the sentence because he begged for it to be halved). May his days be few, may his job be given to someone else (7). When he is dead may his orphans be beggars (9). May he look in vain for anyone in the world to pity him (11). Let God always remember against him the sins of his parents (13). Even more devilish in one verse is the otherwise beautiful 137 where a blessing is pronounced on anyone who will snatch up a Babylonian baby and beat its brains out against the pavement (9). And we get the refinement of malice in 69, 23, " Let their table be made a snare to take themselves withal; and let the things that should have been for their wealth be unto them an occasion of falling."

The examples which (in me at any rate) can hardly fail to produce a smile may occur most disquietingly in Psalms we love; 143, after proceeding for eleven verses in a strain that brings tears to the eyes, adds in the twelfth, almost like an afterthought " and of thy goodness slay mine enemies ". Even more naïvely, almost child-ishly, 139, in the middle of its hymn of praise throws in (*19*) " Wilt thou not slay the wicked, O God?"—as if it were surprising that such a simple remedy for human ills had not occurred to the Almighty. Worst of all in " The Lord is my shepherd " (23), after the green pasture, the waters of comfort, the sure confidence in the valley of the shadow, we suddenly run across (5) " Thou shalt prepare a table for me *against them that trouble me* "—or, as Dr. Moffatt translates it, " Thou art my host, spreading a feast for me *while my enemies have to look on.*" The poet's enjoyment of his present prosperity would not be complete unless those horrid enemies (who used to look down their noses at him) were watching it all and hating it. This may not be so diabolical as the passages I have quoted above; but the pettiness and vulgarity of it, especially in such surroundings, are hard to endure.

One way of dealing with these terrible or (dare we say?) contemptible Psalms is simply to leave them alone. But unfortunately the bad parts will not " come away clean "; they may, as we have noticed, be intertwined with the most exquisite things. And if we still believe that all Holy Scripture is " written for our learning " or that the age-old use of the Psalms in Christian worship was not entirely contrary to the will of God, and if we remember that Our Lord's mind and language were clearly steeped in the Psalter, we shall prefer, if possible, to make some use of them. What use can be made?

Part of the answer to this question cannot be given until we come to consider the subject of allegory. For the moment I can only describe, on the chance that it may help others, the use which I have, undesignedly and gradually, come to make of them myself.

At the outset I felt sure, and I feel sure still, that we must not either try to explain them away or to yield for one moment to the idea that, because it comes in the Bible, all this vindictive hatred must somehow be good and pious. We must face both facts squarely. The hatred is there—festering, gloating, undisguised—and also we should be wicked if we in any way condoned or approved it, or (worse still) used it to justify similar passions in ourselves. Only after these two admissions have been made can we safely proceed.

The first thing that helped me—this is a common experience—came from an angle that did not seem to be religious at all. I found that these maledictions were in one way extremely interesting. For here one saw a feeling we all know only too well, Resentment, expressing itself with perfect freedom, without disguise, without self-consciousness, without shame—as few but children would express it to-day. I did not of course think that this was because the ancient Hebrews had no conventions or restraints. Ancient and oriental cultures are in many ways more conventional, more ceremonious, and more courteous than our own. But their restraints came in different places. Hatred did not need to be disguised for the sake of social decorum or for fear anyone would accuse you of a neurosis. We therefore see it in its " wild " or natural condition.

One might have expected that this would immediately, and usefully, have turned my attention to the same thing in my own heart. And that, no doubt, is one very good use we can make of the maledictory Psalms. To be sure, the hates which we fight against in ourselves do not dream of quite such appalling revenges. We live—at least, in some countries we still live—in a milder age. These poets lived in a world of savage punishments, of massacre and violence, of blood sacrifice in all countries and human sacrifice in many. And of course, too, we are far more subtle than they in disguising our ill will from others and from ourselves. " Well," we say, " he'll live to be sorry for it," as if we were merely, even regretfully, predicting; not noticing, certainly not admitting, that what we predict gives us a certain satisfaction. Still more in the Psalmists' tendency to chew over and over the cud of some injury, to dwell in a kind of self-torture on every circumstance that aggravates it, most of us can recognise something we have met in ourselves. We are, after all, blood-brothers to these ferocious, self-pitying, barbaric men.

That, as I say, is a good use to make of the cursings. In fact, however, something else occurred to me first. It seemed to me that, seeing in them hatred undisguised, I saw also the natural result of injuring a human being. The word *natural* is here important. This result can be obliterated by grace, suppressed by prudence or social convention, and (which is dangerous) wholly disguised by self-deception. But just as the natural result of throwing a lighted match into a pile of shavings is to produce a fire—though damp or the intervention of some more sensible person may prevent it—so the natural result of cheating a man, or "keeping him down" or neglecting him, is to arouse resentment; that is, to impose upon him the temptation of becoming what the Psalmists were when they wrote the vindictive passages. He may succeed in resisting the temptation; or he may not. If he fails, if he dies spiritually because of his hatred for me, how do I, who provoked that hatred, stand? For in addition to the original injury I have done him a far worse one. I have introduced into his inner life, at best a new temptation, at worst a new besetting sin. If that sin utterly corrupts him, I have in a sense debauched or seduced him. I was the tempter.

There is no use talking as if forgiveness were easy. We all know the old joke, "You've given up smoking once; I've given it up a dozen times." In the same way I could say of a certain man, "Have I forgiven him for what he did that day? I've forgiven him more times than I can count." For we find that the work of forgiveness has to be done over and over again. We forgive, we mortify our resentment; a week later some chain of thought

carries us back to the original offence and we discover
the old resentment blazing away as if nothing had been
done about it at all. We need to forgive our brother
seventy times seven not only for 490 offences but for
one offence. Thus the man I am thinking of has introduced a new, and difficult temptation into a soul which
had the devil's plenty of them already. And what he has
done to me, doubtless I have done to others; I, who am
exceptionally blessed in having been allowed a way of
life in which, having little power, I have had little oppor-
tunity of oppressing and embittering others. Let all of us
who have never been school prefects, N.C.O.s, school-
masters, matrons of hospitals, prison warders, or even
magistrates, give hearty thanks for it.

It is monstrously simple-minded to read the cursings
in the Psalms with no feeling except one of horror at the
uncharity of the poets. They are indeed devilish. But
we must also think of those who made them so. Their
hatreds are the reaction to something. Such hatreds are
the kind of thing that cruelty and injustice, by a sort of
natural law, produce. This, among other things, is what
wrong-doing means. Take from a man his freedom or
his goods and you may have taken his innocence, almost
his humanity, as well. Not all the victims go and hang
themselves like Mr. Pilgrim; they may live and hate.

Then another thought occurred which led me in an
unexpected, and at first unwelcome, direction. The reaction of the Psalmists to injury, though profoundly
natural, is profoundly wrong. One may try to excuse it
on the ground that they were not Christians and knew no
better. But there are two reasons why this defence,
though it will go some way, will not go very far.

The first is that within Judaism itself the corrective
to this natural reaction already existed. " Thou shalt not
hate thy brother in thine heart . . . thou shalt not avenge
or bear any grudge against the children of thy people,
but thou shalt love thy neighbour as thyself," says
Leviticus (19, *17, 18*). In *Exodus* we read, " If thou seest

the ass of him that hateth thee lying under his burden
... thou shalt surely help with him," and " if thou meet
thine enemy's ox or his ass going astray, thou shalt surely
bring it back to him " (23, *4, 5*). " Rejoice not when
thine enemy falleth, and let not thine heart be glad
when he stumbleth " (*Proverbs* 24, *17*). And I shall
never forget my surprise when I first discovered that St.
Paul's " If thine enemy hunger, give him bread ", etc., is
a direct quotation from the same book (*Proverbs* 25, *21*).
But this is one of the rewards of reading the Old Testament regularly. You keep on discovering more and more
what a tissue of quotations from it the New Testament
is; how constantly Our Lord repeated, reinforced, continued, refined, and sublimated, the Judaic ethics, how
very seldom He introduced a novelty. This indeed was
perfectly well known—was almost axiomatic—to millions
of unlearned Christians as long as Bible-reading was
habitual. Nowadays it seems to be so forgotten that
people think they have somehow discredited Our Lord if
they can show that some pre-Christian document (or
what they take to be pre-Christian) such as the Dead Sea
Scrolls has " anticipated " Him. As if we supposed Him
to be a cheapjack, like Nietzsche, inventing a new ethic !
Every good teacher, within Judaism as without, has anticipated Him. The whole religious history of the pre-
Christian world, on its better side, anticipates Him. It
could not be otherwise. The Light which has lightened
every man from the beginning may shine more clearly
but cannot change. The Origin cannot suddenly start
being, in the popular sense of the word, " original ".

The second reason is more disquieting. If we are to
excuse the poets of the Psalms on the ground that they
were not Christians, we ought to be able to point to the
same sort of thing, and worse, in Pagan authors. Perhaps
if I knew more Pagan literature I should be able to do
this. But in what I do know (a little Greek, a little Latin,
and of Old Norse very little indeed) I am not at all sure

that I can. I can find in them lasciviousness, much brutal insensibility, cold cruelties taken for granted, but not this fury or luxury of hatred. I mean, of course, where writers are speaking in their own person; speeches put into the mouths of angry characters in a play are a different matter. One's first impression is that the Jews were much more vindictive and vitriolic than the Pagans.

If we are not Christians we shall dismiss this with the old gibe "How odd of God to choose the Jews". That is impossible for us who believe that God chose that race for the vehicle of His own Incarnation, and who are indebted to Israel beyond all possible repayment.

Where we find a difficulty we may always expect that a discovery awaits us. Where there is cover we hope for game. This particular difficulty is well worth exploring.

It seems that there is a general rule in the moral universe which may be formulated "The higher, the more in danger". The "average sensual man" who is sometimes unfaithful to his wife, sometimes tipsy, always a little selfish, now and then (within the law) a trifle sharp in his deals, is certainly, by ordinary standards, a "lower" type than the man whose soul is filled with some great Cause, to which he will subordinate his appetites, his fortune, and even his safety. But it is out of the second man that something really fiendish can be made; an Inquisitor, a Member of the Committee of Public Safety. It is great men, potential saints, not little men, who become merciless fanatics. Those who are readiest to die for a cause may easily become those who are readiest to kill for it. One sees the same principle at work in a field (comparatively) so unimportant as literary criticism; the most brutal work, the most rankling hatred of all other critics and of nearly all authors, may come from the most honest and disinterested critic, the man who cares most passionately and selflessly about literature. The higher the stakes, the greater the temptation to lose your temper over the game. We must not overvalue the relative harmlessness of the little, sensual, frivolous people. They are not above, but below, some temptations.

If I am never tempted, and cannot even imagine myself being tempted, to gamble, this does not mean that I am better than those who are. The timidity and pessimism which exempt me from that temptation themselves tempt me to draw back from those risks and adventures which every man ought to take. In the same way we cannot be certain that the comparative absence of vindictiveness in the Pagans, though certainly a good thing in itself, is a good symptom. This was borne in upon me during a night journey taken early in the Second War in a compartment full of young soldiers. Their conversation made it clear that they totally disbelieved all that they had read in the papers about the wholesale cruelties of the Nazi *régime*. They took it for granted, without argument, that this was all lies, all propaganda put out by our own government to " pep up " our troops. And the shattering thing was, that, believing this, they expressed not the slightest anger. That our rulers should falsely attribute the worst of crimes to some of their fellow-men in order to induce other men to shed their blood seemed to them a matter of course. They weren't even particularly interested. They saw nothing wrong in it. Now it seemed to me that the most violent of the Psalmists—or, for that matter any child wailing out " But it's not fair "—was in a more hopeful condition than these young men. If they had perceived, and felt as a man should feel, the diabolical wickedness which they believed our rulers to be committing, and then forgiven them, they would have been saints. But not to perceive it at all—not even to be tempted to resentment—to accept it as the most ordinary thing in the world—argues a terrifying insensibility. Clearly these young men had (on that subject anyway) no conception of good and evil whatsoever.

Thus the absence of anger, especially that sort of anger which we call *indignation*, can, in my opinion, be a most alarming symptom. And the presence of indignation may be a good one. Even when that indignation passes into bitter personal vindictiveness, it may still be a good symptom, though bad in itself. It is a sin; but it at least shows that those who commit it have not sunk below the level at which the temptation to that sin exists—just as the sins (often quite appalling) of the great patriot or great reformer point to something in him above mere self. If the Jews cursed more bitterly than the Pagans this was, I think, at least in part because they took right and wrong more seriously. For if we look at their railings we find they are usually angry not simply because these things have been done to them but because these things are manifestly wrong, are hateful to God as well as to the victim. The thought of the " righteous Lord "— who surely must hate such doings as much as they do, who surely therefore must (but how terribly He delays!) " judge " or avenge, is always there, if only in the background. Sometimes it comes into the foreground; as in 58, *9, 10,* " The righteous shall rejoice when he seeth the vengeance . . . so that a man shall say . . . Doubtless there is a God that judgeth the earth." This is something different from mere anger without indignation—the almost animal rage at finding that a man's enemy has done to him exactly what he would have done to his enemy if he had been strong enough or quick enough.

Different, certainly higher, a better symptom; yet also leading to a more terrible sin. For it encourages a man to think that his own worst passions are holy. It encourages him to add, explicitly or implicitly, " Thus saith the Lord " to the expression of his own emotions or even his own opinions; as Carlyle and Kipling and some politicians, and even, in their own way, some modern critics, so horribly do. (It is this, by the way, rather than mere idle " profane swearing " that we ought to mean by " taking God's name in vain ". The man who says " Damn that chair!" does not really wish that it should first be endowed with an immortal soul and then sent to

eternal perdition.) For here also it is true " the higher,
the more in danger ". The Jews sinned in this matter
worse than the Pagans not because they were further
from God but because they were nearer to Him. For the
Supernatural, entering a human soul, opens to it new
possibilities both of good and evil. From that point the
road branches : one way to sanctity, love, humility, the
other to spiritual pride, self-righteousness, persecuting
zeal. And no way back to the mere humdrum virtues
and vices of the unawakened soul. If the Divine call does
not make us better, it will make us very much worse. Of
all bad men religious bad men are the worst. Of all
created beings the wickedest is one who originally stood
in the immediate presence of God. There seems no way
out of this. It gives a new application to Our Lord's
words about " counting the cost ".

For we can still see, in the worst of their maledictions,
how these old poets were, in a sense, near to God.
Though hideously distorted by the human instrument,
something of the Divine voice can be heard in these
passages. Not, we trust, that God looks upon their
enemies as they do : He " desireth not the death of a
sinner ". But doubtless He has for the sin of those
enemies just the implacable hostility which the poets
express. Implacable? Yes, not to the sinner but to sin.
It will not be tolerated nor condoned, no treaty will be
made with it. That tooth must come out, that right hand
must be amputated, if the man is to be saved. In that
way the relentlessness of the Psalmists is far nearer to one
side of the truth than many modern attitudes which can
be mistaken, by those who hold them, for Christian
charity. It is, for example, obviously nearer than the
total moral indifference of the young soldiers. It is
nearer than the pseudo-scientific tolerance which reduces
all wickedness to neurosis (though of course some apparent wickedness is). It even contains a streak of sanity
absent from the old woman presiding at a juvenile court
who—I heard it myself—told some young hooligans,

convicted of a well-planned robbery for gain (they had already sold the swag and some had previous convictions against them) that they must, they really must, give up such "stupid pranks". Against all this the ferocious parts of the Psalms serve as a reminder that there is in the world such a thing as wickedness and that it (if not its perpetrators) is hateful to God. In that way, however dangerous the human distortion may be, His word sounds through these passages too.

But can we, besides learning from these terrible Psalms, also use them in our devotional life? I believe we can; but that topic must be reserved for a later chapter.

IV

DEATH IN THE PSALMS

ACCORDING TO my policy of taking first what is most unattractive, I should now proceed to the self-righteousness in many of the Psalms. But we cannot deal with that properly until some other matters have been noticed. I turn first to a very different subject.

Our ancestors seem to have read the Psalms and the rest of the Old Testament under the impression that the authors wrote with a pretty full understanding of Christian Theology; the main difference being that the Incarnation, which for us is something recorded, was for them something predicted. In particular, they seldom doubted that the old authors were, like ourselves, concerned with a life beyond death, that they feared damnation and hoped for eternal joy.

In our own Prayer Book version, and probably in many others, some passages make this impression almost irresistibly. Thus in 17, *14*, we read of wicked men " which have their portion in this life ". The Christian reader inevitably reads into this (and Coverdale, the translator, obviously did so too) Our Lord's contrast between the Rich Man who had his good things here and Lazarus who had them hereafter; the same contrast which is implied in Luke 6, *24*—" Woe unto you that are rich, for ye have received your consolation." But modern translators can find nothing like this in the actual Hebrew. In reality this passage is merely one of the cursings we were considering in the previous chapter. In 17, *13* the poet prays God to " cast down " (in Dr. Moffatt, " crush ") the ungodly; in verse *14*, a refinement occurs to him. Yes, crush them, but first let them

34

" have their portion in this life ". Kill them, but first give
them a bad time while alive.

Again, in 49, we have " No man may deliver his
brother . . . for it cost more to redeem their souls; so that
he must let that alone forever " (7, 8). Who would not
think that this referred to the redeeming work of Christ?
No man can " save " the soul of another. The price of
salvation is one that only the Son of God could pay; as
the hymn says, there was no other " good enough to pay
the price ". The very phrasing of our version strengthens
the effect—the verb " redeem " which (outside the pawn-
broking business) is now used only in a theological sense,
and the past tense of " cost ". Not it " costs ", but it did
cost, more, once and for all on Calvary. But apparently
the Hebrew poet meant something quite different and
much more ordinary. He means merely that death is
inevitable. As Dr. Moffatt translates it : " None can buy
himself off. Not one can purchase for a price from God
(soul's ransom is too dear) life that shall never end."

At this point I can imagine a lifelong lover of the
Psalms exclaiming : " Oh bother the great scholars and
modern translators ! I'm not going to let them spoil the
whole Bible for me. At least let me ask two questions.
(i) Is it not stretching the arm of coincidence rather far
to ask me to believe that, not once but twice, in the same
book, mere accident (wrong translations, bad manu-
scripts, or what not) should have so successfully imitated
the language of Christianity? (ii) Do you mean that the
old meanings which we have always attached to these
verses simply have to be scrapped?" Both questions will
come up for consideration in a later chapter. For the
moment I will only say that, to the second, my personal
answer is a confident No. I return to what I believe to be
the facts.

It seems quite clear that in most parts of the Old
Testament there is little or no belief in a future life; certainly no belief that is of any religious importance. The
word translated " soul " in our version of the Psalms

means simply " life "; the word translated "hell" means
simply " the land of the dead ", the state of all the dead,
good and bad alike, *Sheol.*

It is difficult to know how an ancient Jew thought
of *Sheol.* He did not like thinking about it. His religion
did not encourage him to think about it. No good could
come of thinking about it. Evil might. It was a
condition from which very wicked people like the
Witch of Endor were believed to be able to conjure
up a ghost. But the ghost told you nothing about Sheol;
it was called up solely to tell you things about our own
world. Or again, if you allowed yourself an unhealthy
interest in Sheol you might be lured into one of the
neighbouring forms of Paganism and " eat the offerings
of the dead " (106, *28*).

Behind all this one can discern a conception not speci-
fically Jewish but common to many ancient religions.
The Greek Hades is the most familiar example to modern
people. Hades is neither Heaven nor Hell; it is almost
nothing. I am speaking of the popular beliefs; of course
philosophers like Plato have a vivid and positive doctrine
of immortality. And of course poets may write fantasies
about the world of the dead. These have often no more
to do with the real Pagan religion than the fantasies we
may write about other planets have to do with real
astronomy. In real Pagan belief, Hades was hardly worth
talking about; a world of shadows, of decay. Homer
(probably far closer to actual beliefs than the later and
more sophisticated poets) represents the ghosts as witless.
They gibber meaninglessly until some living man gives
them sacrificial blood to drink. How the Greeks felt
about it in his time is startlingly shown at the beginning
of the *Iliad* where he says of men killed in battle that
" their souls " went to Hades but " the men themselves "
were devoured by dogs and carrion birds. It is the body,
even the dead body which is the man himself; the ghost
is only a sort of reflection or echo. (The grim impulse

sometimes has crossed my mind to wonder whether all this was, is, in fact true; that the merely natural fate of humanity, the fate of unredeemed humanity, is just this —to disintegrate in soul as in body, to be a witless psychic sediment. If so, Homer's idea that only a drink of sacrificial blood can restore a ghost to rationality would be one of the most striking among many Pagan anticipations of the truth.)

Such a conception, vague and marginal even in Paganism, becomes more so in Judaism. Sheol is even dimmer, further in the background, than Hades. It is a thousand miles away from the centre of Jewish religion; especially in the Psalms. They speak of Sheol (or " hell " or " the pit ") very much as a man speaks of " death " or " the grave " who has no belief in any sort of future state whatever—a man to whom the dead are simply dead, nothing, and there's no more to be said.

In many passages this is quite clear, even in our translation, to every attentive reader. The clearest of all is the cry in 89, *46* : " O remember how short my time is : why hast thou made all men for nought?" We all come to nothing in the end. Therefore " every man living is altogether vanity " (39, *6*). Wise and foolish have the same fate (49, *10*). Once dead, a man worships God no more; " Shall the dust give thanks unto thee?" (30, *10*); " for in death no man remembereth thee " (6, *5*). Death is " the land " where, not only worldly things, but all things, " are forgotten " (88, *12*). When a man dies " all his thoughts perish " (146, *3*). Every man will " follow the generation of his fathers, and shall never see light " (49, *19*) : he goes into a darkness which will never end.

Elsewhere, I admit, it sounds as if the poet were praying for the " salvation of his soul " in the Christian sense. Almost certainly he is not. In 30, *3*, " Thou hast brought my soul out of hell " means " you have saved me from death ". " The snares of death compassed me round about, and the pains of hell gat hold upon me " (116, *3*) means "Death was setting snares for me, I felt the anguish of a dying man "—as we should say, "I was at death's door."

As we all know from our New Testaments, Judaism had greatly changed in this respect by Our Lord's time. The Sadducees held to the old view. The Pharisees, and apparently many more, believed in the life of the world to come. When, and by what stages, and (under God) from what sources, this new belief crept in, is not part of our present subject. I am more concerned to try to understand the absence of such a belief, in the midst of intense religious feeling, over the earlier period. To some it may seem astonishing that God, having revealed so much of Himself to that people, should not have taught them this.

It does not now astonish me. For one thing there were nations close to the Jews whose religion was overwhelmingly concerned with the after life. In reading about ancient Egypt one gets the impression of a culture in which the main business of life was the attempt to secure the well-being of the dead. It looks as if God did not want the chosen people to follow that example. We may ask why. Is it possible for men to be too much concerned with their eternal destiny? In one sense, paradoxical though it sounds, I should reply, Yes.

For the truth seems to me to be that happiness or misery beyond death, simply in themselves, are not even religious subjects at all. A man who believes in them will of course be prudent to seek the one and avoid the other. But that seems to have no more to do with religion than looking after one's health or saving money for one's old age. The only difference here is that the stakes are so very much higher. And this means that, granted a real and steady conviction, the hopes and anxieties aroused are overwhelming. But they are not on that account the more religious. They are hopes for oneself, anxieties for oneself. God is not in the centre. He is still important only for the sake of something else. Indeed such a belief can exist without a belief in God at all. Buddhists are much concerned with what will happen to them after death, but are not, in any true sense, Theists.

It is surely, therefore, very possible that when God began to reveal Himself to men, to show them that He and nothing else is their true goal and the satisfaction of their needs, and that He has a claim upon them simply by being what He is, quite apart from anything He can bestow or deny, it may have been absolutely necessary that this revelation should not begin with any hint of future Beatitude or Perdition. These are not the right points to begin at. An effective belief in them, coming too soon, may even render almost impossible the development of (so to call it) the appetite for God; personal hopes and fears, too obviously exciting, have got in first. Later, when, after centuries of spiritual training, men have learned to desire and adore God, to pant after Him " as pants the hart ", it is another matter. For then those who love God will desire not only to enjoy Him but " to enjoy Him forever ", and will fear to lose Him. And it is by that door that a truly religious hope of Heaven and fear of Hell can enter; as corollaries to a faith already centred upon God, not as things of any independent or intrinsic weight. It is even arguable that the moment " Heaven " ceases to mean union with God and " Hell " to mean separation from Him, the belief in either is a mischievous superstition; for then we have, on the one hand, a merely " compensatory " belief (a " sequel " to life's sad story, in which everything will " come all right ") and, on the other, a nightmare which drives men into asylums or makes them persecutors.

Fortunately, by God's good providence, a strong and steady belief of that self-seeking and sub-religious kind is extremely difficult to maintain, and is perhaps possible only to those who are slightly neurotic. Most of us find that our belief in the future life is strong only when God is in the centre of our thoughts; that if we try to use the hope of " Heaven " as a compensation (even for the most innocent and natural misery, that of bereavement) it crumbles away. It can, on those terms, be maintained only by arduous efforts of controlled imagination; and we know in our hearts that the imagination is our own. As for Hell, I have often been struck, in reading the " hell-fire sermons " of our older divines, at the desperate efforts they make to render these horrors vivid to their hearers, at their astonishment that men, with such horrors hanging over them, can live as carelessly as they do. But perhaps it is not really astonishing. Perhaps the divines are appealing, on the level of self-centred prudence and self-centred terror, to a belief which, on that level, cannot really exist as a permanent influence on conduct—though doubtless it may be worked up for a few excited minutes or even hours.

All this is only one man's opinion. And it may be unduly influenced by my own experience. For I (I have said it in another book, but the repetition is unavoidable) was allowed for a whole year to believe in God and try—in some stumbling fashion—to obey Him before any belief in the future life was given me. And that year always seems to me to have been of very great value. It is therefore perhaps natural that I should suspect a similar value in the centuries during which the Jews were in the same position. Other views no doubt can be taken.

Of course among ancient Jews, as among us, there were many levels. They were not all of them, not perhaps any of them at all times, disinterested, any more than we. What then filled the place which was later taken by the hope of Heaven (too often, I am afraid, desired chiefly as an escape from Hell) was of course the hope of peace and plenty on earth. This was in itself no less (but really no more) sub-religious than prudential cares about the next world. It was not quite so personal and self-centred as our own wishes for earthly prosperity. The individual, as such, seems to have been less aware of himself, much less separated from others, in those ancient times. He did not so sharply distinguish his own prosperity from that of the nation and especially of his own descendants. Blessings on one's remote posterity were blessings on oneself. Indeed it is not always easy to know whether the speaker in a Psalm is the individual poet or Israel itself. I suspect that sometimes the poet had never raised the question.

But we should be quite mistaken if we supposed that these worldly hopes were the only thing in Judaism. They are not the characteristic thing about it, the thing that sets it apart from ancient religion in general. And notice here the strange roads by which God leads His people. Century after century, by blows which seem to us merciless, by defeat, deportation, and massacre, it was hammered into the Jews that earthly prosperity is not in fact the certain, or even the probable, reward of seeing God. Every hope was disappointed. The lesson taught in the *Book of Job* was grimly illustrated in practice. Such experience would surely have destroyed a religion which had no other centre than the hope of peace and plenty with " every man under his own vine and his own fig tree ". We know that many did " fall off ". But the astonishing thing is that the religion is not destroyed. In its best representatives it grows purer, stronger, and more profound. It is being, by this terrible discipline, directed more and more to its real centre. That will be the subject of the next chapter.

V

"THE FAIR BEAUTY OF THE LORD"

"Now LET us stint all this and speak of mirth." So far
—I couldn't help it—this book has been what the old
woman in Scott described as "a cauld clatter o' morality". At last we can turn to better things. If we think
"mirth" an unsuitable word for them, that may show
how badly we need something which the Psalms can
give us perhaps better than any other book in the
world.

David, we know, danced before the Ark. He danced
with such abandon that one of his wives (presumably a
more modern, though not a better type than he) thought
he was making a fool of himself. David didn't care
whether he was making a fool of himself or not. He was
rejoicing in the Lord. This helps to remind us at the outset that Judaism, though it is the worship of the one true
and eternal God, is an ancient religion. That means that
its externals, and many of its attitudes, were much more
like those of Paganism than they were like all that
stuffiness—all that regimen of tiptoe tread and lowered
voice—which the word "religion" suggests to so many
people now. In one way, of course, this puts a barrier
between it and us. We should not have enjoyed the
ancient rituals. Every temple in the world, the elegant
Parthenon at Athens and the holy Temple at Jerusalem,
was a sacred slaughterhouse. (Even the Jews seem to
shrink from a return to this. They have not rebuilt the
Temple nor revived the sacrifices.) But even that has two
sides. If temples smelled of blood, they also smelled of
roast meat; they struck a festive and homely note, as well
as a sacred.

When I read the Bible as a boy I got the idea that the

Temple of Jerusalem was related to the local synagogues very much as a great cathedral is related to the parish churches in a Christian country. In reality there is no such parallel. What happened in the synagogues was quite unlike what happened in the Temple. The synagogues were meeting-houses where the Law was read and where an address might be given—often by some distinguished visitor (as in *Luke* 4, *20* or *Acts* 13, *15*). The Temple was the place of sacrifice, the place where the essential worship of Jahveh was enacted. Every parish church is the descendant of both. By its sermons and lessons it shows its ancestry in the synagogue. But because the Eucharist is celebrated and all other sacraments administered in it, it is like the Temple; it is a place where the adoration of the Deity can be fully enacted. Judaism without the Temple was mutilated, deprived of its central operation; any church, barn, sickroom, or field, can be the Christian's temple.

The most valuable thing the Psalms do for me is to express that same delight in God which made David dance. I am not saying that this is so pure or so profound a thing as the love of God reached by the greatest Christian saints and mystics. But I am not comparing it with that, I am comparing it with the merely dutiful "churchgoing" and laborious "saying our prayers" to which most of us are, thank God not always, but often, reduced. Against that it stands out as something astonishingly robust, virile, and spontaneous; something we may regard with an innocent envy and may hope to be infected by as we read.

For the reason I have given, this delight is very much centred on the Temple. The simpler poets do not in fact distinguish between the love of God in what we might (rather dangerously) call "a spiritual sense" and their enjoyment of the festivals in the Temple. We must not misunderstand this. The Jews were not, like the Greeks, an analytical and logical people; indeed, except the Greeks, no ancient peoples were. The sort of distinction

which we can easily make between those who are really
worshipping God in church and those who enjoy "a
beautiful service" for musical, antiquarian, or merely
sentimental reasons, would have been impossible to them.
We get nearest to their state of mind if we think of a
pious modern farm-labourer at church on Christmas
Day or at the harvest thanksgiving. I mean, of course,
one who really believes, who is a regular communicant;
not one who goes only on these occasions and is thus (not
in the worst but in the best sense of that word) a Pagan,
practising Pagan piety, making his bow to the Unknown
—and at other times Forgotten—on the great annual
festivals. The man I picture is a real Christian. But you
would do him wrong by asking him to separate out,
at such moments, some exclusively religious element in
his mind from all the rest—from his hearty social pleasure in a corporate act, his enjoyment of the hymns (and
the crowd), his memory of other such services since
childhood, his well-earned anticipation of rest after
harvest or Christmas dinner after church. They are all
one in his mind. This would have been even truer of any
ancient man, and especially of an ancient Jew. He was a
peasant, very close to the soil. He had never heard of
music, or festivity, or agriculture as things separate from
religion, nor of religion as something separate from
them. Life was one. This assuredly laid him open to
spiritual dangers which more sophisticated people can
avoid; it also gave him privileges which they lack.

Thus when the Psalmists speak of "seeing" the Lord,
or long to "see" Him, most of them mean something
that happened to them in the Temple. The fatal way of
putting this would be to say "they only mean they have
seen the festival". It would be better to say "If we had
been there we should have seen only the festival". Thus
in 68 "It is well seen, O God, how thou goest[1] . . . in the
sanctuary . . . the singers go before, the minstrels follow

[1] This was perhaps sung while the Ark itself was carried
round.

after; in the midst are the damsels playing with the timbrels " (24-25), it is almost as if the poet said " Look, here He comes ". If I had been there I should have seen the musicians and the girls with the tambourines; in addition, as another thing, I might or might not have (as we say) " felt " the presence of God. The ancient worshipper would have been aware of no such dualism. Similarly, if a modern man wished to " dwell in the house of the Lord all the days of his life, to behold the fair beauty of the Lord " (27, 4) he would mean, I suppose, that he hoped to receive, not of course without the mediation of the sacraments and the help of other " services ", but as something distinguishable from them and not to be presumed upon as their inevitable result, frequent moments of spiritual vision and the " sensible " love of God. But I suspect that the poet of that Psalm drew no distinction between " beholding the fair beauty of the Lord " and the acts of worship themselves.

When the mind becomes more capable of abstraction and analysis this old unity breaks up. And no sooner is it possible to distinguish the rite from the vision of God than there is a danger of the rite becoming a substitute for, and a rival to, God Himself. Once it can be thought of separately, it will; and it may then take on a rebellious, cancerous life of its own. There is a stage in a child's life at which it cannot separate the religious from the merely festal character of Christmas or Easter. I have been told of a very small and very devout boy who was heard murmuring to himself on Easter morning a poem of his own composition which began " Chocolate eggs and Jesus risen ". This seems to me, for his age, both admirable poetry and admirable piety. But of course the time will soon come when such a child can no longer effortlessly and spontaneously enjoy that unity. He will become able to distinguish the spiritual from the ritual and festal aspect of Easter; chocolate eggs will no longer be sacramental. And once he has distinguished he must put one or the other first. If he puts the spiritual first he can still taste something of Easter in the chocolate eggs; if he puts the eggs first they will soon be no more than any other sweetmeat. They have taken on an independent, and therefore a soon withering, life. Either at some period in Judaism, or else in the experience of some Jews, a roughly parallel situation occurred. The unity falls apart; the sacrificial rites become distinguishable from the meeting with God. This does not unfortunately mean that they will cease or become less important. They may, in various evil modes, become even more important than before. They may be valued as a sort of commercial transaction with a greedy God who somehow really wants or needs large quantities of carcasses and whose favours cannot be secured on any other terms. Worse still, they may be regarded as the only thing He wants, so that their punctual performance will satisfy Him without obedience to His demands for mercy, "judgement", and truth. To the priests themselves the whole system will seem important simply because it is both their art and their livelihood; all their pedantry, all their pride, all their economic position, is bound up with it. They will elaborate their art more and more. And of course the corrective to these views of sacrifice can be found within Judaism itself. The prophets continually fulminate against it. Even the Psalter, though largely a Temple collection, can do so; as in Psalm 50 where God tells His people that all this Temple worship, considered in itself, is not the real point at all, and particularly ridicules the genuinely Pagan notion that He really needs to be fed with roast meat. "If I were hungry, do you think I would apply to *you*?" (*12*). I have sometimes fancied He might similarly ask a certain type of modern clergyman, "If I wanted music—if I were conducting research into the more recondite details of the history of the Western Rite—do you really think *you* are the source I would rely on?"

This possible degradation of sacrifice and the rebukes of it are, however, so well known that there is no need to stress them here. I want to stress what I think that we (or at least I) need more; the joy and delight in God which meet us in the Psalms, however loosely or closely, in this or that instance, they may be connected with the Temple. This is the living centre of Judaism. These poets knew far less reason than we for loving God. They did not know that He offered them eternal joy; still less that He would die to win it for them. Yet they express a longing for Him, for His mere presence, which comes only to the best Christians or to Christians in their best moments. They long to live all their days in the Temple so that they may constantly see " the fair beauty of the Lord " (27, 4). Their longing to go up to Jerusalem and " appear before the presence of God " is like a physical thirst (42). From Jerusalem His presence flashes out " in perfect beauty " (50, 2). Lacking that encounter with Him, their souls are parched like a waterless countryside (63, 2). They crave to be " satisfied with the pleasures " of His house (65, 4). Only there can they be at ease, like a bird in the nest (84, 3). One day of those " pleasures " is better than a lifetime spent elsewhere (10).

I have rather—though the expression may seem harsh to some—called this the " appetite for God " than " the love of God ". The " love of God " too easily suggests the word " spiritual " in all those negative or restrictive senses which it has unhappily acquired. These old poets do not seem to think that they are meritorious or pious for having such feelings; nor, on the other hand, that they are privileged in being given the grace to have them. They are at once less priggish about it than the worst of us and less humble—one might almost say, less surprised—than the best of us. It has all the cheerful spontaneity of a natural, even a physical, desire. It is gay and jocund. They are glad and rejoice (9, 2). Their fingers itch for the harp (43, 4), for the lute and the harp —wake up, lute and harp!—(57, 9); let's have a song, bring the tambourine, bring the " merry harp with the lute ", we're going to sing merrily and make a cheerful noise (81, *1*, 2). Noise, you may well say. Mere music is not enough. Let everyone, even the benighted gentiles,[1] clap their hands (47, *1*). Let us have clashing cymbals, not only well tuned, but *loud*, and dances too (150, *5*). Let even the remote islands (all islands were remote, for the Jews were no sailors) share the exultation (97, *1*).

I am not saying that this gusto—if you like, this rowdiness—can or should be revived. Some of it cannot be revived because it is not dead but with us still. It would be idle to pretend that we Anglicans are a striking example. The Romans, the Orthodox, and the Salvation Army all, I think, have retained more of it than we. We have a terrible concern about good taste. Yet even we can still exult. The second reason goes far deeper. All Christians know something the Jews did not know about what it " cost to redeem their souls ". Our life as Christians begins by being baptised into a death; our most joyous festivals begin with, and centre upon, the broken body and the shed blood. There is thus a tragic depth in our worship which Judaism lacked. Our joy has to be the sort of joy which can coexist with that; there is for us a spiritual counterpoint where they had simple melody. But this does not in the least cancel the delighted debt which I, for one, feel that I owe to the most jocund Psalms. There, despite the presence of elements we should now find it hard to regard as religious at all, and the absence of elements which some might think essential to religion, I find an experience fully God-centred, asking of God no gift more urgently than His presence, the gift of Himself, joyous to the highest degree, and unmistakably real. What I see (so to speak) in the faces of these old poets tells me more about the God whom they and we adore.

But this characteristically Hebraic delight or gusto finds also another channel. We must follow it in the next chapter.

---

[1] Not "all ye people" as in our version, but "all ye nations" (*Goyim*).

VI

"SWEETER THAN HONEY"

IN RACINE's tragedy of *Athalie* the chorus of Jewish girls
sing an ode about the original giving of the Law on
Mount Sinai, which has the remarkable refrain *ô charmante loi* (Act 1, scene iv). Of course it will not do—it
will border on the comic—to translate this " oh charming
Law ". *Charming* in English has come to be a tepid and
even patronising word; we use it of a pretty cottage, of a
book that is something less than great or a woman who is
something less than beautiful. How we should translate
charmante I don't know; " enchanting?"—" delightful?"—" beautiful?" None of them quite fits. What is,
however, certain is that Racine (a mighty poet and
steeped in the Bible) is here coming nearer than any
modern writer I know to a feeling very characteristic of
certain Psalms. And it is a feeling which I at first found
utterly bewildering.

" More to be desired are they than gold, yea than
much fine gold : sweeter also than honey and the honeycomb " (19, *10*). One can well understand this being said
of God's mercies, God's visitations, His attributes. But
what the poet is actually talking about is God's law, His
commands; His " rulings " as Dr. Moffatt well translates
in verse *9* (for " judgements " here plainly means deci-
sions about conduct). What is being compared to gold
and honey is those " statutes " (in the Latin version
" decrees ") which, we are told, " rejoice the heart " (*8*).
For the whole poem is about the Law, not about
" judgement " in the sense to which Chapter I was
devoted.

This was to me at first very mysterious. " Thou shalt
not steal, thou shalt not commit adultery "—I can under-

stand that a man can, and must, respect these "statutes", and try to obey them, and assent to them in his heart. But it is very hard to find how they could be, so to speak, delicious, how they exhilarate. If this is difficult at any time, it is doubly so when obedience to either is opposed to some strong, and perhaps *in itself* innocent, desire. A man held back by his unfortunate previous marriage to some lunatic or criminal who never dies from some woman whom he faithfully loves, or a hungry man left alone, without money, in a shop filled with the smell and sight of new bread, roasting coffee, or fresh strawberries—can these find the prohibition of adultery or of theft at all like honey? They may obey, they may still respect the "statute". But surely it could be more aptly compared to the dentist's forceps or the front line than to anything enjoyable and sweet.

A fine Christian and a great scholar to whom I once put this question said he thought that the poets were referring to the satisfaction men felt in knowing they had obeyed the Law; in other words, to the "pleasures of a good conscience". They would, on his view, be meaning something very like what Wordsworth meant when he said we know nothing more beautiful than the "smile" on Duty's face—her smile when her orders have been carried out. It is rash for me to differ from such a man, and his view certainly makes excellent sense. The difficulty is that the Psalmists never seem to me to say anything very like this.

In 1, 2 we are told that the good man's "delight is in the law of the Lord, and in his law will he exercise himself day and night". To "exercise himself" in it apparently does not mean to obey it (though no doubt the good man will do that too) but to study it, as Dr. Moffatt says to "pore over it". Of course "the Law" does not here mean simply the ten commandments, it means the whole complex legislation (religious, moral, civil, criminal and even constitutional) contained in *Leviticus, Numbers* and *Deuteronomy*. The man who "pores upon it." is obeying Joshua's command (*Joshua* 1, 8), "the book of the Law shall not depart out of thy mouth; but thou shalt meditate therein day and night." This means, among other things, that the Law was a study or, as we should say, a "subject"; a thing on which there would be commentaries, lectures, and examinations. There were. Thus part (religiously, the least important part) of what an ancient Jew meant when he said he "delighted in the Law" was very like what one of us would mean if he said that somebody "loved" history, or physics, or archaeology. This might imply a wholly innocent—though, of course, merely natural—delight in one's favourite subject; or, on the other hand, the pleasures of conceit, pride in one's own learning and consequent contempt for the outsiders who don't share it, or even a venal admiration for the studies which secure one's own stipend and social position.

The danger of this second development is obviously increased tenfold when the study in question is from the outset stamped as sacred. For then the danger of spiritual pride is added to that of mere ordinary pedantry and conceit. One is sometimes (not often) glad not to be a great theologian; one might so easily mistake it for being a good Christian. The temptations to which a great philologist or a great chemist is exposed are trivial in comparison. When the subject is sacred, proud and clever men may come to think that the outsiders who don't know it are not merely inferior to them in skill but lower in God's eyes; as the priests said (*John* 7, 49), "All that rabble who are not experts in the Torah are accursed." And as this pride increases, the "subject" or study which confers such privilege will grow more and more complicated, the list of things forbidden will increase, till to get through a single day without supposed sin becomes like an elaborate step-dance, and this horrible network breeds self-righteousness in some and haunting anxiety in others. Meanwhile the "weightier matters of the Law", righteousness itself, shrinks into insignificance under this vast overgrowth, so that the legalists strain at a gnat and swallow a camel.

Thus the Law, like the sacrifice, can take on a cancerous life of its own and work against the thing for whose sake it existed. As Charles Williams wrote, " When the means are autonomous they are deadly." This morbid condition of the Law contributed to—I do not suggest it is the sole or main cause of—St. Paul's joyous sense of Christ as the Deliverer from Law. It is against this same morbid condition that Our Lord uttered some of His sternest words; it is the sin, and simultaneously the punishment, of the Scribes and Pharisees. But that is not the side of the matter I want to stress here, nor does it by this time need stressing. I would rather let the Psalms show me again the good thing of which this bad thing is the corruption.

As everyone knows, the Psalm specially devoted to the Law is 119, the longest in the whole collection. And everyone has probably noticed that from the literary or technical point of view, it is the most formal and elaborate of them all. The technique consists in taking a series of words which are all, for purposes of this poem, more or less synonyms (*word, statutes, commandments, testimonies,* etc.), and ringing the changes on them through each of its eight-verse sections—which themselves correspond to the letters of the alphabet. (This may have given an ancient ear something of the same sort of pleasure we get from the Italian metre called the *Sestina,* where instead of rhymes we have the same end words repeated in varying orders in each stanza.) In other words, this poem is not, and does not pretend to be, a sudden outpouring of the heart like, say, Psalm 18. It is a pattern, a thing done like embroidery, stitch by stitch, through long, quiet hours, for love of the subject and for the delight in leisurely, disciplined craftsmanship.

Now this, in itself, seems to me very important because it lets us into the mind and mood of the poet. We can guess at once that he felt about the Law somewhat as

he felt about his poetry; both involved exact and lovi͟
conformity to an intricate pattern. This at once suggests
an attitude from which the Pharisaic conception could
later grow but which in itself, though not necessarily
religious, is quite innocent. It will look like priggery or
pedantry (or else like a neurotic fussiness) to those who
cannot sympathise with it, but it need not be any of these
things. It may be the delight in Order, the pleasure in
getting a thing "just so"—as in dancing a minuet. Of
course the poet is well aware that something incompar-
ably more serious than a minuet is here in question. He
is also aware that he is very unlikely, himself, to achieve
this perfection of discipline : "O that my ways *were*
made so straight that I *might* keep thy statutes !" (*5*).
At present they aren't, and he can't. But his effort to do
so does not spring from servile fear. The Order of the
Divine mind, embodied in the Divine Law, is beautiful.
What should a man do but try to reproduce it, so far as
possible, in his daily life? His "delight" is in those
statutes (*16*); to study them is like finding treasure (*14*);
they affect him like music, are his "songs" (*54*); they
taste like honey (*103*); they are better than silver and
gold (*72*). As one's eyes are more and more opened, one *
sees more and more in them, and it excites wonder (*18*).
This is not priggery nor even scrupulosity; it is the language of a man ravished by a moral beauty. If we cannot
at all share his experience, we shall be the losers. Yet I
cannot help fancying that a Chinese Christian—one
whose own traditional culture had been the "schoolmaster to bring him to Christ"—would appreciate this
Psalm more than most of us; for it is an old idea in that
culture that life should above all things be ordered and
that its order should reproduce a Divine order.

But there is something else to our purpose in this
grave poem. On three occasions the poet asserts that the
Law is "true" or "the truth" (*86, 138, 142*). We find
the same in 111, 7, "all his commandments are true".
(The word, I understand, could also be translated "faith-

ful ", or " sound "; what is, in the Hebrew sense, " true "
is what " holds water ", what doesn't " give way " or col-
lapse.) A modern logician would say that the Law is a
command and that to call a command " true " makes no
sense; " The door is shut " may be true or false but
" Shut the door " can't. But I think we all see pretty well
what the Psalmists mean. They mean that in the Law
you find the " real " or " correct " or stable, well-
grounded, directions for living. The law answers the
question " Wherewithal shall a young man cleanse his
way?" (119, 9). It is like a lamp, a guide (105). There
are many rival directions for living, as the Pagan cultures
all round us show. When the poets call the directions or
" rulings " of Jahveh " true " they are expressing the
assurance that these, and not those others, are the " real "
or " valid " or unassailable ones; that they are based on
the very nature of things and the very nature of God.

By this assurance they put themselves, implicitly, on
the right side of a controversy which arose far later
among Christians. There were in the eighteenth century
terrible theologians who held that " God did not command certain things because they are right, but certain
things are right because God commanded them ". To
make the position perfectly clear, one of them even said
that though God has, as it happens, commanded us to
love Him and one another, He might equally well have
commanded us to hate Him and one another, and hatred
would then have been right. It was apparently a mere
toss-up which He decided on. Such a view in effect
makes God a mere arbitrary tyrant. It would be better
and less irreligious to believe in no God and to have no
ethics than to have such an ethics and such a theology
as this. The Jews of course never discuss this in abstract
and philosophical terms. But at once, and completely,
they assume the right view, knowing better than they
know. They know that the Lord (not merely obedience
to the Lord) is " righteous " and commands " righteousness " because He loves it (11, 8). He enjoins what is

good because it is good, because He is good. Hence His laws have *emeth* " truth ", intrinsic validity, rock-bottom reality, being rooted in His own nature, and are therefore as solid as that Nature which He has created. But the Psalmists themselves can say it best; " thy righteousness standeth like the strong mountains, thy judgements are like the great deep " (36, 6).[1] Their delight in the Law is a delight in having touched firmness; like the pedestrian's delight in feeling the hard road beneath his feet after a false short cut has long entangled him in muddy fields.

For there were other roads, which lacked " truth ". The Jews had as their immediate neighbours, close to them in race as well as in position, Pagans of the worst kind, Pagans whose religion was marked by none of that beauty or (sometimes) wisdom which we can find among the Greeks. That background made the " beauty " or " sweetness " of the Law more visible; not least because these neighbouring Paganisms were a constant temptation to the Jew and may in some of their externals have been not unlike his own religion. The temptation was to turn to those terrible rites in times of terror— when, for example, the Assyrians were pressing on. We who not so long ago waited daily for invasion by enemies, like the Assyrians, skilled and constant in systematic cruelty, know how they may have felt. They were tempted, since the Lord seemed deaf, to try those appalling deities who demanded so much more and might therefore perhaps give more in return. But when a Jew in some happier hour, or a better Jew even in that hour, looked at those worships—when he thought of sacred prostitution, sacred sodomy, and the babies thrown into the fire for Moloch—his own " Law " as he turned back to it must have shone with an extraordinary radiance. Sweeter than honey; or if that metaphor does not suit us who have not such a sweet tooth as all ancient peoples (partly because we have plenty of sugar), let us say like

[1] See Appendix I, p. 117.

mountain water, like fresh air after a dungeon, like sanity after a nightmare. But, once again, the best image is in a Psalm, the 19th.[1]

I take this to be the greatest poem in the Psalter and one of the greatest lyrics in the world. Most readers will remember its structure; six verses about Nature, five about Law, and four of personal prayer. The actual words supply no logical connection between the first and second movements. In this way its technique resembles that of the most modern poetry. A modern poet would pass with similar abruptness from one theme to another and leave you to find out the connecting link for yourself. But then he would possibly be doing this quite deliberately; he might have, though he chose to conceal, a perfectly clear and conscious link in his own mind which he could express to you in logical prose if he wanted to. I doubt if the ancient poet was like that. I think he felt, effortlessly and without reflecting on it, so close a connection, indeed (for his imagination) such an identity, between his first theme and his second that he passed from the one to the other without realising that he had made any transition. First he thinks of the sky; how, day after day, the pageantry we see there shows us the splendour of its Creator. Then he thinks of the sun, the bridal joyousness of its rising, the unimaginable speed of its daily voyage from east to west. Finally, of its heat; not of course the mild heats of our climate but the cloudless, blinding, tyrannous rays hammering the hills, searching every cranny. The key phrase on which the whole poem depends is " there is nothing hid from the heat thereof ". It pierces everywhere with its strong, clean ardour. Then at once, in verse 7 he is talking of something else, which hardly seems to him something else because it is so like the all-piercing, all-detecting sunshine. The Law is " undefiled ", the Law gives light, it is clean and everlasting, it is " sweet ". No one can improve on this and nothing can more fully admit us to the old

[1] See Appendix I, p. 116.

Jewish feeling about the Law; luminous, severe, disinfectant, exultant. One hardly needs to add that this poet is wholly free from self-righteousness and the last section is concerned with his "secret faults". As he has felt the sun, perhaps in the desert, searching him out in every nook of shade where he attempted to hide from it, so he feels the Law searching out all the hiding-places of his soul.

In so far as this idea of the Law's beauty, sweetness, or preciousness, arose from the contrast of the surrounding Paganisms, we may soon find occasion to recover it. Christians increasingly live on a spiritual island; new and rival ways of life surround it in all directions and their tides come further up the beach every time. None of these new ways is yet so filthy or cruel as some Semitic Paganism. But many of them ignore all individual rights and are already cruel enough. Some give morality a wholly new meaning which we cannot accept, some deny its possibility. Perhaps we shall all learn, sharply enough, to value the clean air and "sweet reasonableness" of the Christian ethics which in a more Christian age we might have taken for granted. But of course, if we do, we shall then be exposed to the danger of priggery. We might come to "thank God that we are not as other men". This introduces the greatest difficulty which the Psalms have raised in my mind.

VII

CONNIVANCE

EVERY ATTENTIVE reader of the Psalms will have noticed that they speak to us severely not merely about doing evil ourselves but about something else. In 26, *4*, the good man is not only free from " vanity " (falsehood) but has not even " dwelled with ", been on intimate terms with, those who are " vain ". He has " hated " them (*5*). So in 31, *7*, he has " hated " idolaters. In 50, *18*, God blames a man not for being a thief but for " consenting to " a thief (in Dr. Moffatt, " you are a friend to any thief you see "). In 141, *4-6*, where our translation appears to be rather wrong, the general sense nevertheless comes through and expresses the same attitude. Almost comically the Psalmist of 139 asks " Don't I hate those who hate thee, Lord? . . . Why, I hate them as if they were *my* enemies ! " (*21. 22*).

Now obviously all this—taking upon oneself to hate those whom one thinks God's enemies, avoiding the society of those one thinks wicked, judging our neighbours, thinking oneself " too good " for some of them (not in the snobbish way, which is a trivial sin in comparison, but in the deepest meaning of the words " too good ")—is an extremely dangerous, almost a fatal, game. It leads straight to " Pharisaism " in the sense which Our Lord's own teaching has given to that word. It leads not only to the wickedness but to the absurdity of those who in later times came to be called the " unco guid ". This I assume from the outset, and I think that even in the Psalms this evil is already at work. But we must not be Pharisaical even to the Pharisees. It is foolish to read such passages without realising that a quite

genuine problem is involved. And I am not at all confident about the solution.

We hear it said again and again that the editor of some
newspaper is a rascal, that some politician is a liar, that
some official person is a tyrannical Jack-in-office and even
dishonest, that someone has treated his wife abominably,
that some celebrity (film-star, author, or what not) leads
a most vile and mischievous life. And the general rule in
modern society is that no one refuses to meet any of
these people and to behave towards them in the friend-
liest and most cordial manner. People will even go out
of their way to meet them. They will not even stop buy-
ing the rascally newspaper, thus paying the owner for the
lies, the detestable intrusions upon private life and private
tragedy, the blasphemies and the pornography, which
they profess to condemn.

I have said there is a problem here, but there are really
two. One is social and almost political. It may be asked
whether that state of society in which rascality undergoes
no social penalty is a healthy one; whether we should
not be a happier country if certain important people
were pariahs as the hangman once was—blackballed at
every club, dropped by every acquaintance, and liable to
the print of riding-crop or fingers across the face if they
were ever bold enough to speak to a respectable woman.
It leads into the larger question whether the great evil of
our civil life is not the fact that there seems now no
medium between hopeless submission and full-dress
revolution. Rioting has died out, moderate rioting. It
can be argued that if the windows of various ministries
and newspapers were more often broken, if certain
people were more often put under pumps and (mildly—
mud, not stones) pelted in the streets, we should get on a
great deal better. It is not wholly desirable that any man
should be allowed at once the pleasures of a tyrant or a
wolf's-head and also those of an honest freeman among
his equals. To this question I do not know the answer.

The dangers of a change in the direction I have outlined are very great; so are the evils of our present tameness.

I am concerned here only with the problem that appears in our individual and private lives. How ought we to behave in the presence of very bad people? I will limit this by changing " very bad people " to " very bad people who are powerful, prosperous and impenitent ". If they are outcasts, poor and miserable, whose wickedness obviously has not " paid ", then every Christian knows the answer. Christ speaking to the Samaritan woman at the well, Christ with the woman taken in adultery, Christ dining with publicans, is our example. I mean, of course, that His humility, His love, His total indifference to the social discredit and misrepresentation He might incur are examples for us; not, Heaven knows, that any of us who was not specially qualified to do so by priesthood, age, old acquaintance, or the earnest request of the sinners themselves, could without insolence and presumption assume the least trace of His authority to rebuke and pardon. (One has to be very careful lest the desire to patronise and the itch to be a busybody should disguise itself as a vocation to help the " fallen ", or tend to obscure our knowledge that we are fallen—perhaps in God's eyes far more so—ourselves.) But we may be sure there were others who equally consorted with " publicans and sinners " and whose motives were very unlike those of Our Lord.

The publicans were the lowest members of what may be called the Vichy or Collaborationist movement in Palestine; men who fleeced their fellow-countrymen to get money for the occupying power in return for a fat percentage of the swag. As such they were like the hangman, outside all decent social intercourse. But some of them did pretty well financially, and no doubt most of them enjoyed, up to a point, the protection and contemptuous favours of the Roman government. One may guess that some consorted with them for very bad reasons —to get " pickings ", to be on good terms with such

dangerous neighbours. Besides Our Lord there would
have been among their guests toadies and those who
wanted to be " on the band-wagon "; people in fact like
a young man I once knew.

He had been a strict socialist at Oxford. Everything
ought to be run by the State; private enterprise and
independent professions were for him the great evil. He
then went away and became a schoolmaster. After about
ten years of that he came to see me. He said his political
views had been wholly reversed. You never heard a fuller
recantation. He now saw that State interference was
fatal. What had converted him was his experience as a
schoolmaster of the Ministry of Education—a set of
ignorant meddlers armed with insufferable powers to
pester, hamper and interrupt the work of real, practical
teachers who knew the subjects they taught, who knew
boys, parents, and all the real conditions of their work.
It makes no difference to the point of the story whether
you agree with his view of the Ministry; the important
thing is that he held that view. For the real point of the
story, and of his visit, when it came, nearly took my
breath away. Thinking thus, he had come to see whether
I had any influence which might help him to get a job in
the Ministry of Education.

Here is the perfect band-wagoner. Immediately on
the decision " This is a revolting tyranny ", follows the
question " How can I as quickly as possible cease to be
one of the victims and become one of the tyrants?" If I
had been able to introduce the young man to someone in
the Ministry, I think we may be sure that his manners
to that hated " meddler " would have been genial and
friendly in the extreme. Thus someone who had heard
his previous invective against the meddling and then wit-
nessed his actual behaviour to the meddler, might possibly
(for charity " believeth all things ") have concluded that
this young man was full of the purest Christianity and
loved one he thought a sinner while hating what he
thought his sin.

Of course this is an instance of band-wagoning so crude and unabashed as to be farcical. Not many of us perhaps commit the like. But there are subtler, more social or intellectual forms of band-wagoning which might deceive us. Many people have a very strong desire to meet celebrated or "important" people, including those whom they disapprove, from curiosity or vanity. It gives them something to talk or even (anyone may produce a book of reminiscences) to write about. It is felt to confer distinction if the great, though odious, man recognises you in the street. And where such motives are in play it is better still to know him quite well, to be intimate with him. It would be delightful if he shouted out "Hallo Bill" while you were walking down the Strand with an impressionable country cousin. I don't know that the desire is itself a very serious defect. But I am inclined to think a Christian would be wise to avoid, where he decently can, any meeting with people who are bullies, lascivious, cruel, dishonest, spiteful and so forth.

Not because we are "too good" for them. In a sense because we are not good enough. We are not good enough to cope with all the temptations, nor clever enough to cope with all the problems, which an evening spent in such society produces. The temptation is to condone, to connive at; by our words, looks and laughter, to "consent". The temptation was never greater than now when we are all (and very rightly) so afraid of priggery or "smugness". And of course, even if we do not seek them out, we shall constantly be in such company whether we wish it or not. This is the real and unavoidable difficulty.

We shall hear vile stories told as funny; not merely licentious stories but (to me far more serious and less noticed) stories which the teller could not be telling unless he was betraying someone's confidence. We shall hear infamous detraction of the absent, often disguised as pity or humour. Things we hold sacred will be mocked. Cruelty will be slyly advocated by the assumption that its

only opposite is "sentimentality". The very presup-
positions of any possible good life—all disinterested
motives, all heroism, all genuing forgiveness—will be,
not explicitly denied (for then the matter could be dis-
cussed), but assumed to be phantasmal, idiotic, believed in
only by children.

What is one to do? For on the one hand, quite
certainly, there is a degree of unprotesting participation
in such talk which is very bad. We are strengthening the
hands of the enemy. We are encouraging him to believe
that "those Christians", once you get them off their
guard and round a dinner table, really think and feel
exactly as he does. By implication we are denying our
Master; behaving as if we "knew not the Man". On
the other hand is one to show that, like Queen Victoria,
one is "not amused"? Is one to be contentious, inter-
rupting the flow of conversation at every moment with
"I don't agree, I don't agree"? Or rise and go away?
But by these courses we may also confirm some of their
worst suspicions of "those Christians". We are just the
sort of ill-mannered prigs they always said.

Silence is a good refuge. People will not notice it
nearly so easily as we tend to suppose. And (better still)
few of us enjoy it as we might be in danger of enjoying
more forcible methods. Disagreement can, I think, sometimes be expressed without the appearance of priggery,
if it is done argumentatively not dictatorially; support
will often come from some most unlikely member of the
party, or from more than one, till we discover that those
who were silently dissentient were actually a majority. A
discussion of real interest may follow. Of course the
right side may be defeated in it. That matters very
much less than I used to think. The very man who
has argued you down will sometimes be found, years
later, to have been influenced by what you said.

There comes, however, a degree of evil against which
a protest will have to be made, however little chance it
has of success. There are cheery agreements in cynicism

or brutality which one must contract out of unambiguously. If it can't be done without seeming priggish, then priggish we must seem.

For what really matters is not seeming but being a prig. If we sufficiently dislike making the protest, if we are strongly tempted not to, we are unlikely to be priggish in reality. Those who positively enjoy, as they call it, "testifying" are in a different and more dangerous position. As for the mere seeming—well, though it is very bad to be a prig, there are social atmospheres so foul that in them it is almost an alarming symptom if a man has never been called one. Just in the same way, though pedantry is a folly and snobbery a vice, yet there are circles in which only a man indifferent to all accuracy will escape being called a pedant, and others where manners are so coarse, flashy and shameless that a man (whatever his social position) of any natural good taste will be called a snob.

What makes this contact with wicked people so difficult is that to handle the situation successfully requires not merely good intentions, even with humility and courage thrown in; it may call for social and even intellectual talents which God has not given us. It is therefore not self-righteousness but mere prudence to avoid it when we can. The Psalmists were not quite wrong when they described the good man as avoiding "the seat of the scornful" and fearing to consort with the ungodly lest he should "eat of" (shall we say, laugh at, admire, approve, justify?) "such things as please them". As usual in their attitude, with all its dangers, there is a core of very good sense. "Lead us not into temptation" often means, among other things, "Deny me those gratifying invitations, those highly interesting contacts, that participation in the brilliant movements of our age, which I so often, at such risk, desire."

Closely connected with these warnings against what I have called "connivance" are the protests of the

Psalter[1] against other sins of the tongue. I think that
when I began to read it these surprised me a little; I had
half expected that in a simpler and more violent age
when more evil was done with the knife, the big stick,
and the firebrand, less would be done by talk. But in
reality the Psalmists mention hardly any kind of evil more
often than this one, which the most civilised societies
share. " Their throat is an open sepulchre, they flat-
ter " (5, *10*), " under his tongue is ungodliness and
vanity ", or " perjury " as Dr. Moffatt translates it (10,
7), " deceitful lips " (12, *3*), " lying lips " (31, *20*), " words
full of deceit " (36, *3*), the " whispering " of evil men (41,
7), cruel lies that " cut like a razor " (52, *3*), talk that
sounds " smooth as oil " and will wound like a sword
(55, *22*), pitiless jeering (102, *8*). It is all over the
Psalter. One almost hears the incessant whispering,
tattling, lying, scolding, flattery, and circulation of
rumours. No historical readjustments are here required,
we are in the world we know. We even detect in that
muttering and wheedling chorus voices which are
familiar. One of them may be too familiar for recognition.

[1] Some of these probably involve archaic, and even magical,
ideas of a power intrinsic in words themselves, so that all blessings and cursings would be efficacious.

VIII

NATURE

TWO FACTORS determine the Psalmists' approach to
Nature. The first they share with the vast majority of
ancient writers; the second was in their time, if not absolutely unique, extremely rare.

i. They belong to a nation chiefly of peasants. For us
the very name Jew is associated with finance, shop-
keeping, money-lending and the like. This however,
dates from the Middle Ages when the Jews were not
allowed to own land and were driven into occupations
remote from the soil. Whatever characteristics the
modern Jew has acquired from millenia of such occupations, they cannot have been those of his ancient ancestors. Those were peasants or farmers. When even a
king covets a piece of his neighbour's property, the piece
is a vineyard; he is more like a wicked squire than a
wicked king. Everyone was close to the land; everyone
vividly aware of our dependence on soils and weather.
So, till a late age, was every Greek and Roman. Thus
part of what we should now, perhaps, call " appreciation
of Nature " could not then exist—all that part which is
really delight in " the country " as a contrast to the town.
Where towns are few and very small and where nearly
everyone is on the land, one is not aware of any special
thing called " the country ". Hence a certain sort of
" nature poetry " never existed in the ancient world till
really vast cities like Alexandria arose; and, after the fall
of ancient civilisation, it never existed again until the
eighteenth century. At other periods what we call " the
country " is simply the world, what water is to a fish.
Nevertheless appreciation of Nature can exist; a delight
which is both utilitarian and poetic. Homer can enjoy a

landscape, but what he means by a beautiful landscape is one that is useful—good deep soil, plenty of fresh water, pasture that will make the cows really fat, and some nice timber. Being one of a seafaring race he adds, as a Jew would not, a good harbour. The Psalmists, who are writing lyrics not romances, naturally give us little landscape. What they do give us, far more sensuously and delightedly than anything I have seen in Greek, is the very feel of weather—weather seen with a real countryman's eyes, enjoyed almost as a vegetable might be supposed to enjoy it. " Thou art good to the earth . . . thou waterest her furrows . . . thou makest it soft with drops of rain . . . the little hills shall rejoice on every side . . . the valleys shall stand so thick with corn that they shall laugh and sing " (65, *9-14*). In 104, *16* (better in Dr. Moffatt than in the Prayer Book), " the great trees drink their fill ".

ii. The Jews, as we all know, believed in one God, maker of heaven and earth. Nature and God were distinct; the One had made the other; the One ruled and the other obeyed. This, I say, we all know. But for various reasons its real significance can easily escape a modern reader if his studies happen not to have led him in certain directions.

In the first place it is for us a platitude. We take it for granted. Indeed I suspect that many people assume that some clear doctrine of creation underlies all religions : that in Paganism the gods, or one of the gods, usually created the world; even that religions normally begin by answering the question, "Who made the world?" In reality, creation, in any unambiguous sense, seems to be a surprisingly rare doctrine; and when stories about it occur in Paganism they are often religiously unimportant, not in the least central to the religions in which we find them. They are on the fringe where religion tails off into what was perhaps felt, even at the time, to be more like fairy-tale. In one Egyptian story a god called Atum came up out of the water and, being apparently a hermaphrodite, begot and bore the two next gods; after that, things could get on. In another, the whole senate of the gods came up out of Nun, the Deep. According to a Babylonian myth, before heaven and earth were made a being called Apsu begot, and a being called Tiamat bore, Lahmu and Lahamu, who in their turn produced Anshar and Kishar. We are expressly told that this pair were greater than their parents, so that it is more like a myth of evolution than of creation. In the Norse myth we begin with ice and fire, and indeed with a north and south, amidst all which, somehow, a giant comes to life, who bears (from his arm-pit) a son and daughter. Greek mythology starts with heaven and earth already in existence.

I do not mention these myths to indulge in a cheap laugh at their crudity. All our language about such things, that of the theologian as well as that of the child, is crude. The real point is that the myths, even in their own terms, do not reach the idea of Creation in our sense at all. Things " come up out of " something or " are formed in " something. If the stories could, for the moment, be supposed true, they would still be stories about very early events in a process of development, a world-history, which was already going on. When the curtain rises in these myths there are always some " properties " already on the stage and some sort of drama is proceeding. You may say they answer the question " How did the play begin?" But that is an ambiguous question. Asked by the man who arrived ten minutes late it would be properly answered, say, with the words, " Oh, first three witches came in, and then there was a scene between an old king and a wounded soldier." That is the sort of question the myths are in fact answering. But the very different question: " How does a play originate? Does it write itself? Do the actors make it up as they go along? Or is there someone—not on the stage, not like the people on the stage—someone we don't see

—who invented it all and caused it to be?"—this is rarely asked or answered.

Admittedly we find in Plato a clear Theology of Creation in the Judaic and Christian sense; the whole universe—the very conditions of time and space under which it exists—are produced by the will of a perfect, timeless, unconditioned God who is above and outside all that He makes. But this is an amazing leap (though not made without the help of Him who is the Father of lights) by an overwhelming theological genius; it is not ordinary Pagan religion.

Now we all understand of course the importance of this peculiarity in Judaic thought from a strictly and obviously religious point of view. But its total consequences, the ways in which it changes a man's whole mind and imagination, might escape us.

To say that God created Nature, while it brings God and Nature into relation, also separates them. What makes and what is made must be two, not one. Thus the doctrine of Creation in one sense empties Nature of divinity. How very hard this was to do and, still more, to keep on doing, we do not now easily realise. A passage from *Job* (not without its own wild poetry in it) may help us. " If I beheld the sun when it shined, or the moon walking in brightness; and my heart hath been secretly enticed, or my mouth kissed my hand; this also would be an iniquity " (31, *26-28*). There is here no question of turning, in a time of desperate need, to devilish gods. The speaker is obviously referring to an utterly spontaneous impulse, a thing you might find yourself acting upon almost unawares. To pay some reverence to the sun or moon is apparently so natural; so apparently innocent. Perhaps in certain times and places it was really innocent. I would gladly believe that the gesture of homage offered to the moon was sometimes accepted by her Maker; in those times of ignorance which God " winked at " (*Acts* 17, *30*). The author of Job, however, was not

in that ignorance. If he had kissed his hand to the Moon
it would have been iniquity. The impulse was a temptation; one which no European has felt for the last thousand years.

But in another sense the same doctrine which empties
Nature of her divinity also makes her an index, a symbol,
a manifestation, of the Divine. I must recall two passages quoted in an earlier chapter. One is that from
Psalm 19 where the searching and cleansing sun becomes
an image of the searching and cleansing Law. The other
is from 36 : " Thy mercy, O Lord, reacheth unto the
heavens, and thy faithfulness unto the clouds. Thy
righteousness standeth like the strong mountains, thy
judgements are like the great deep " (5, 6). It is surely
just because the natural objects are no longer taken to be
themselves Divine that they can now be magnificent
symbols of Divinity. There is little point in comparing a
Sun-god with the Sun or Neptune with the great deep;
there is much in comparing the Law with the Sun or
saying that God's judgements are an abyss and a mystery
like the sea.

But of course the doctrine of Creation leaves Nature
full of manifestations which show the presence of God,
and created energies which serve Him. The light is His
garment, the thing we partially see Him through (104, 2),
the thunder can be His voice (29, 3-5). He dwells in the
dark thundercloud (18, 11), the eruption of a volcano
comes in answer to His touch (104, 32). The world is
full of his emissaries and executors. He makes winds His
messengers and flames His servants(104, 4), rides upon
cherubim (18, 10), commands the army of angels.

All this is clearly in one way very close to Paganism.
Thor and Zeus also spoke in the thunder; Hermes or Iris
was the messenger of the gods. But the difference, though
subtle, is momentous, between hearing in the thunder the
voice of God or the voice of a god. As we have seen, even
in the creation-myths, gods have beginnings. Most of

them have fathers and mothers; often we know their
birth-places. There is no question of self-existence or the
timeless. Being is imposed upon them, as upon us, by
preceding causes. They are, like us, creatures or products; though they are luckier than we in being stronger,
more beautiful, and exempt from death. They are, like
us, actors in the cosmic drama, not its authors. Plato fully
understood this. His God creates the gods and preserves
them from death by His own power; they have no inher-
ent immortality. In other words, the difference between
believing in God and in many gods is not one of arith-
metic. As someone has said " gods " is not really the
plural of God; God has no plural. Thus, when you hear
in the thunder the voice of a god, you are stopping short,
for the voice of a god is not really a voice from beyond
the world, from the uncreated. By taking the god's voice
away—or envisaging the god as an angel, a servant of
that Other—you go further. The thunder becomes not
less divine but more. By emptying Nature of divinity—
or, let us say, of divinities—you may fill her with Deity,
for she is now the bearer of messages. There is a sense in
which Nature-worship silences her—as if a child or a
savage were so impressed with the postman's uniform
that he omitted to take in the letters.

Another result of believing in Creation is to see
Nature not as a mere datum but as an achievement.
Some of the Psalmists are delighted with its mere solidity
and permanence. God has given to His works His own
character of *emeth*; they are watertight, faithful, reliable,
not at all vague or phantasmal. "All His works are
faithful—He spake and it was done, He commanded and
it stood fast " (33, *4, 9*). By His might (Dr. Moffatt's
version) " the mountains are made firm and strongly
fixed " (65, *6*). God has laid the foundations of the
earth with perfect thoroughness (104, *5*). He has made
everything firm and permanent and imposed boundaries
which limit each thing's operation (148, *6*). Notice how

in Psalm 136 the poet passes from God's creation of
Nature to the delivering of Israel out of Egypt : both are
equally great deeds, great victories.

But the most surprising result of all is still to be mentioned. I said that the Jews, like nearly all the ancients,
were agricultural and approached Nature with a garden-
er's and a farmer's interest, concerned with rain, with
grass " for the service of man ", wine to cheer man up
and olive-oil to make his face shine—to make it look, as
Homer says somewhere, like a peeled onion (104, *14, 15*).
But we find them led on beyond this. Their gusto, or
even gratitude, embraces things that are no use to man.
In the great Psalm especially devoted to Nature, from
which I have just quoted (104),[1] we have not only the
useful cattle, the cheering vine, and the nourishing corn.
We have springs where the wild asses quench their thirst
(*11*), fir trees for the storks (*17*), hill country for the wild
goats and " conies " (perhaps marmots, *18*), finally even
the lions (*21*); and even with a glance far out to sea,
where no Jew willingly went, the great whales playing,
enjoying themselves (*26*).

Of course this appreciation of, almost this sympathy
with, creatures useless or hurtful or wholly irrelevant to
man, is not our modern " kindness to animals ". That is
a virtue most easily practised by those who have never,
tired and hungry, had to work with animals for a bare
living, and who inhabit a country where all dangerous
wild beasts have been exterminated.[2] The Jewish feeling,
however, is vivid, fresh, and impartial. In Norse stories
a pestilent creature such as a dragon tends to be conceived as the enemy not only of men but of gods. In
classical stories, more disquietingly, it tends to be sent by

---

[1] See Appendix I, p. 123.
[2] Heaven forbid, however, that I should be thought to slight it.
I only mean that for those of us who meet beasts solely as pets it
is not a costly virtue. We may properly be kicked if we lack it,
but must not pat ourselves on the back for having it. When a
hard-worked shepherd or carter remains kind to animals his back
may well be patted; not ours.

a god for the destruction of men whom he has a grudge
against. The Psalmist's clear objective view—noting the
lions and whales side by side with men and men's cattle
—is unusual. And I think it is certainly reached through
the idea of God as Creator and sustainer of all. In 104,
21, the point about the lions is that they, like us, "do
seek their meat from God". All these creatures, like us,
"wait upon" God at feeding-time (27). It is the same in
147, 9; though the raven was an unclean bird to Jews,
God "feedeth the young ravens that call upon him".
The thought which gives these creatures a place in the
Psalmist's gusto for Nature is surely obvious. They are
our fellow-dependents; we all, lions, storks, ravens,
whales—live, as our fathers said, "at God's charges",
and mention of all equally redounds to His praise.

One curious bit of evidence strengthens my belief that
there is such a connection between this sort of nature
poetry and the doctrine of creation; and it is also so
interesting in itself that I think it worth a digression. I
have said that Paganism in general fails to get out of
nature something that the Jews got. There is one apparent instance to the contrary; one ancient Gentile
poem which provides a fairly close parallel to Psalm
104. But then, when we come to examine it, we find that
this poem is not Pagan in the sense of Polytheistic at all.
It is addressed to a Monotheistic God and salutes Him as
the Creator of the whole earth. It is therefore no excep-
tion to my generalisation. Where ancient Gentile literature (in some measure) anticipates the nature poetry of
the Jews, it has also (in some measure) anticipated their
theology. And that, in my view, is what we might have
expected.

The poem in question is an Egyptian *Hymn to the Sun*
dating from the fourteenth century B.C. Its author is
that Pharaoh whose real name was Amenhetep IV, but
who called himself Akhenaten. Many of my readers
will know his story already. He was a spiritual revolu-
tionary. He broke away from the Polytheism of his

fathers and nearly tore Egypt into shreds in his efforts to establish by force the worship of a single God. In the eyes of the established priesthood, whose property he transferred to the service of this new religion, he must have seemed a monster; a sort of Henry VIII plundering the abbeys. His Monotheism appears to have been of an extremely pure and conceptual kind. He did not, as a man of that age might have been expected to do, even identify God with the Sun. The visible disc was only His manifestation. It is an astonishing leap, more astonishing in some ways than Plato's, and, like Plato's, in sharp contrast to ordinary Paganism. And as far as we can see, it was a total failure. Akhenaten's religion died with him. Nothing, apparently, came of it.

Unless of course, as is just possible, Judaism itself partly came of it. It is conceivable that ideas derived from Akhenaten's system formed part of that Egyptian "Wisdom" in which Moses was bred. There is nothing to disquiet us in such a possibility. Whatever was true in Akhenaten's creed came to him, in some mode or other, as all truth comes to all men, from God. There is no reason why traditions descending from Akhenaten should not have been among the instruments which God used in making Himself known to Moses. But we have no evidence that this is what actually happened. Nor do we know how fit Akhenatenism would really have been to serve as an instrument for this purpose. Its inside, its spirituality, the quality of life from which it sprang and which it encouraged, escape us. The man himself still has the power, after thirty-four centuries, to evoke the most violent, and contradictory, reactions. To one modern scholar he is the "first individual" whom history records; to another, he is a crank, a faddist, half insane, possibly cretinous. We may well hope that he was accepted and blessed by God; but that his religion, at any rate on the historical level, was not so blessed and so accepted, is pretty clear. Perhaps the seed was good seed but fell on stony ground. Or perhaps it was not after all exactly the right sort of seed. To us moderns, no doubt, such a simple, enlightened, reasonable Monotheism looks very much more like the good seed than those earliest documents of Judaism in which Jahveh seems little more that a tribal deity. We might be wrong. Perhaps if Man is finally to know the bodiless, timeless, transcendent Ground of the whole universe not as a mere philosophical abstraction but as the Lord who, despite this transcendence, is "not far from any one of us", as an utterly concrete Being (far more concrete than we) whom Man can fear, love, address, and "taste", he must begin far more humbly and far nearer home, with the local altar, the traditional feast, and the treasured memories of God's judgements, promises, and mercies. It is possible that a certain sort of enlightenment can come too soon and too easily. At that early stage it may not be fruitful to typify God by anything so remote, so neutral, so international and (as it were) interdenominational, so featureless, as the solar disc. Since in the end we are to come to baptism and the Eucharist, to the stable at Bethlehem, the hill of Calvary, and the emptied rock-tomb, perhaps it is better to begin with circumcision, the Passover, the Ark, and the Temple. For "the highest does not stand without the lowest". Does not stand, does not stay; rises, rather, and expands, and finally loses itself in endless space. For the entrance is low : we must stoop till we are no taller than children in order to get in.

It would therefore be rash to assume that Akhenaten's Monotheism was, in those ways which are religiously most important, an exact anticipation of the Judaic; so that if only the priests and people of Egypt had accepted it, God could have dispensed with Israel altogether and revealed Himself to us henceforward through a long line of Egyptian prophets. What concerns us at the moment, however, is simply to note that Akhenaten's religion, being certainly in some respects like that of the Jews, sets him free to write nature-poetry in some degree like theirs. The degree could be exaggerated. The *Hymn to the Sun* remains different from the Psalms. It is magnificently like Psalm 139 *(13-16)* when it praises God for making the embryo grow in the mother's body, so that He is " our nurse even in the womb " : or for teaching the chick to break the eggshell and come forth " chirping as loud as he can ". In the verse " Thou didst create the earth, according to thy desire " Akhenaten even anticipates the New Testament—" thou hast created all things, and for thy pleasure they are, and were created " *(Revelation* 4, *11)*. But he does not quite see the lions as our fellow-pensioners. He brings them in, to be sure, but notice how : " when thou settest, the world is in darkness like the dead. Out come the lions : all serpents sting." Thus coupled with death and poisonous snakes, they are clearly envisaged in their capacity of enemies. It almost sounds as if the night itself were an enemy, out of God's reach. There is just a trace of dualism. But if there is difference, the likeness also is real. And it is the likeness which is relevant to the theme of this chapter. In Akhenaten as in the Psalms, a certain kind of poetry seems to go with a certain kind of theology. But the full and abiding development of both is Jewish.

(Meanwhile, what gentle heart can leave the topic without a prayer that this lonely ancient king, crank and doctrinaire though perhaps he was, has long seen and now enjoys the truth which so far transcends his own glimpse of it?)

IX

A WORD ABOUT PRAISING

IT IS POSSIBLE (and it is to be hoped) that this chapter will be unnecessary for most people. Those who were never thick-headed enough to get into the difficulty it deals with may even find it funny. I have not the least objection to their laughing; a little comic relief in a discussion does no harm, however serious the topic may be. (In my own experience the funniest things have occurred in the gravest and most sincere conversations.)

When I first began to draw near to belief in God and even for some time after it had been given to me, I found a stumbling block in the demand so clamorously made by all religious people that we should "praise" God; still more in the suggestion that God Himself demanded it. We all despise the man who demands continued assurance of his own virtue, intelligence or delightfulness; we despise still more the crowd of people round every dictator, every millionaire, every celebrity, who gratify that demand. Thus a picture, at once ludicrous and horrible, both of God and of His worshippers, threatened to appear in my mind. The Psalms were especially troublesome in this way—"Praise the Lord," "O praise the Lord with me," "Praise Him." (And why, incidentally, did praising God so often consist in telling other people to praise Him? Even in telling whales, snowstorms, etc., to go on doing what they would certainly do whether we told them or not?) Worse still was the statement put into God's own mouth, "whoso offereth me thanks and praise, he honoureth me" (50, 23). It was hideously like saying, "What I most want is to be told that I am good and great." Worst of all was the suggestion of the very silliest Pagan bargaining, that

77

of the savage who makes offerings to his idol when the fishing is good and beats it when he has caught nothing. More than once the Psalmists seemed to be saying, " You like praise. Do this for me, and you shall have some." Thus in 54 the poet begins " save me " (*1*), and in verse *6* adds an inducement, " An offering of a free heart will I give thee, and praise thy Name." Again and again the speaker asks to be saved from death on the ground that if God lets His suppliants die He will get no more praise from them, for the ghosts in Sheol cannot praise (30, *10*; 88, *10*; 119, *175*). And mere quantity of praise seemed to count; " seven times a day do I praise thee " (119, *164*). It was extremely distressing. It made one think what one least wanted to think. Gratitude to God, reverence to Him, obedience to Him, I thought I could understand; not this perpetual eulogy. Nor were matters mended by a modern author who talked of God's " right " to be praised.

I still think " right " is a bad way of expressing it, but I believe I now see what the author meant. It is perhaps easiest to begin with inanimate objects which can have no rights. What do we mean when we say that a picture is " admirable "? We certainly don't mean that it is admired (that's as may be) for bad work is admired by thousands and good work may be ignored. Nor that it " deserves " admiration in the sense in which a candidate " deserves " a high mark from the examiners—i.e. that a human being will have suffered injustice if it is not awarded. The sense in which the picture " deserves " or " demands " admiration is rather this; that admiration is the correct, adequate or appropriate, response to it, that, if paid, admiration will not be " thrown away ", and that if we do not admire we shall be stupid, insensible, and great losers, we shall have missed something. In that way many objects both in Nature and in Art may be said to deserve, or merit, or demand, admiration. It was from this end, which will seem to some irreverent, that I found it best to approach the idea that God " demands " praise.

wants us to acknowledge, in truth

He is that Object to admire which (or, if you like, to appreciate which) is simply to be awake, to have entered the real world; not to appreciate which is to have lost the greatest experience, and in the end to have lost all. The incomplete and crippled lives of those who are tone-deaf, have never been in love, never known true friendship, never cared for a good book, never enjoyed the feel of the morning air on their cheeks, never (I am one of these) enjoyed football, are faint images of it.

But of course this is not all. God does not only "demand" praise as the supremely beautiful and all-satisfying Object. He does apparently command it as lawgiver. The Jews were told to sacrifice. We are under an obligation to go to church. But this was a difficulty only because I did not then understand any of what I have tried to say above in Chapter V. I did not see that it is in the process of being worshipped that God communicates His presence to men. It is not indeed the only way. But for many people at many times the "fair beauty of the Lord" is revealed chiefly or only while they worship Him together. Even in Judaism the essence of the sacrifice was not really that men gave bulls and goats to God, but that by their so doing God gave Himself to men; in the central act of our own worship of course this is far clearer—there it is manifestly, even physically, God who gives and we who receive. The miserable idea that God should in any sense need, or crave for, our worship like a vain woman wanting compliments, or a vain author presenting his new books to people who never met or heard of him, is implicitly answered by the words "If I be hungry I will not tell *thee*" (50, *12*). Even if such an absurd Deity could be conceived, He would hardly come to *us*, the lowest of rational creatures, to gratify His appetite. I don't want my dog to bark approval of my books. Now that I come to think of it, there are some humans whose enthusiastically favourable criticism would not much gratify me.

But the most obvious fact about praise—whether of

God or anything—strangely escaped me. I thought of it in terms of compliment, approval, or the giving of honour. I had never noticed that all enjoyment spontaneously overflows into praise unless (sometimes even if) shyness or the fear of boring others is deliberately brought in to check it. The world rings with praise— lovers praising their mistresses, readers their favourite poet, walkers praising the countryside, players praising their favourite game—praise of weather, wines, dishes, actors, motors, horses, colleges, countries, historical personages, children, flowers, mountains, rare stamps, rare beetles, even sometimes politicians or scholars. I had not noticed how the humblest, and at the same time most balanced and capacious, minds, praised most, while the cranks, misfits and malcontents praised least. The good critics found something to praise in many imperfect works; the bad ones continually narrowed the list of books we might be allowed to read. The healthy and unaffected man, even if luxuriously brought up and widely experienced in good cookery, could praise a very modest meal : the dyspeptic and the snob found fault with all. Except where intolerably adverse circumstances interfere, praise almost seems to be inner health made audible. Nor does it cease to be so when, through lack of skill, the forms of its expression are very uncouth or even ridiculous. Heaven knows, many poems of praise addressed to an earthly beloved are as bad as our bad hymns, and an anthology of love poems for public and perpetual use would probably be as sore a trial to literary taste as *Hymns Ancient and Modern.* I had not noticed either that just as men spontaneously praise whatever they value, so they spontaneously urge us to join them in praising it : " Isn't she lovely? Wasn't it glorious? Don't you think that magnificent?" The Psalmists in telling everyone to praise God are doing what all men do when they speak of what they care about. My whole, more general, difficulty about the praise of God depended on my absurdly denying to us,

as regards the supremely Valuable, what we delight to
do, what indeed we can't help doing, about everything
else we value.

I think we delight to praise what we enjoy because the
praise not merely expresses but completes the enjoyment;
it is its appointed consummation. It is not out of compliment that lovers keep on telling one another how beautiful they are; the delight is incomplete till it is expressed.
It is frustrating to have discovered a new author and not
to be able to tell anyone how good he is; to come suddenly, at the turn of the road, upon some mountain valley
of unexpected grandeur and then to have to keep silent
because the people with you care for it no more than for
a tin can in the ditch; to hear a good joke and find no
one to share it with (the perfect hearer died a year ago).
This is so even when our expressions are inadequate, as
of course they usually are. But how if one could really
and fully praise even such things to perfection—utterly
" get out " in poetry or music or paint the upsurge of
appreciation which almost bursts you? Then indeed the
object would be fully appreciated and our delight would
have attained perfect development. The worthier the
object, the more intense this delight would be. If it were
possible for a created soul fully (I mean, up to the full
measure conceivable in a finite being) to " appreciate ",
that is to love and delight in, the worthiest object of all,
and simultaneously at every moment to give this delight
perfect expression, then that soul would be in supreme
beatitude. It is along these lines that I find it easiest to
understand the Christian doctrine that " Heaven " is a
state in which angels now, and men hereafter, are per-
petually employed in praising God. This does not mean,
as it can so dismally suggest, that it is like " being in
Church ". For our " services " both in their conduct and
in our power to participate, are merely attempts at worship; never fully successful, often 99.9 per cent failures,
sometimes total failures. We are not riders but pupils in
the riding school; for most of us the falls and bruises, the

aching muscles and the severity of the exercise, far outweigh those few moments in which we were, to our own astonishment, actually galloping without terror and without disaster. To see what the doctrine really means, we must suppose ourselves to be in perfect love with God— drunk with, drowned in, dissolved by, that delight which, far from remaining pent up within ourselves as incommunicable, hence hardly tolerable, bliss, flows out from us incessantly again in effortless and perfect expression, our joy no more separable from the praise in which it liberates and utters itself than the brightness a mirror receives is separable from the brightness it sheds. The Scotch catechism says that man's chief end is " to glorify God and enjoy Him forever ". But we shall then know that these are the same thing. Fully to enjoy is to glorify. In commanding us to glorify Him, God is inviting us to enjoy Him.

Meanwhile of course we are merely, as Donne says, tuning our instruments. The tuning up of the orchestra can be itself delightful, but only to those who can in some measure, however little, anticipate the symphony. The Jewish sacrifices, and even our own most sacred rites, as they actually occur in human experience, are, like the tuning, promise, not performance. Hence, like the tuning, they may have in them much duty and little delight; or none. But the duty exists for the delight. When we carry out our " religious duties " we are like people digging channels in a waterless land, in order that when at last the water comes, it may find them ready. I mean, for the most part. There are happy moments, even now, when a trickle creeps along the dry beds; and happy souls to whom this happens often.

As for the element of bargaining in the Psalms (Do this and I will praise you), that silly dash of Paganism certainly existed. The flame does not ascend pure from the altar. But the impurities are not its essence. And we are not all in a position to despise even the crudest Psalmists on this score. Of course we would not blunder in our

words like them. But there is, for ill as well as for good,
a wordless prayer. I have often, on my knees, been
shocked to find what sort of thoughts I have, for a
moment, been addressing to God; what infantile placa-
tions I was really offering, what claims I have really
made, even what absurd adjustments or compromises I
was, half-consciously, proposing. There is a Pagan,
savage heart in me somewhere. For unfortunately the
folly and idiot-cunning of Paganism seem to have far
more power of surviving than its innocent or even
beautiful elements. It is easy, once you have power, to
silence the pipes, still the dances, disfigure the statues,
and forget the stories; but not easy to kill the savage,
the greedy, frightened creature now cringing, now
blustering, in one's soul—the creature to whom God
may well say, " thou thoughtest I am even such a one as
thyself " (50, 21).

But all this, as I have said, will be illuminating to
only a few of my readers. To the others, such a comedy
of errors, so circuitous a journey to reach the obvious,
will furnish occasion for charitable laughter.

X

SECOND MEANINGS

I MUST NOW turn to something far more difficult. Hitherto we have been trying to read the Psalms as we suppose—or I suppose—their poets meant them to be read. But this of course is not the way in which they have chiefly been used by Christians. They have been believed to contain a second or hidden meaning, an "allegorical" sense, concerned with the central truths of Christianity, with the Incarnation, the Passion, the Resurrection, the Ascension, and with the Redemption of man. All the Old Testament has been treated in the same way. The full significance of what the writers are saying is, on this view, apparent only in the light of events which happened after they were dead.

Such a doctrine, not without reason, arouses deep distrust in a modern mind. Because, as we know, almost anything can be read into any book if you are determined enough. This will be especially impressed on anyone who has written fantastic fiction. He will find reviewers, both favourable and hostile, reading into his stories all manner of allegorical meanings which he never intended. (Some of the allegories thus imposed on my own books have been so ingenious and interesting that I often wish I had thought of them myself.) Apparently it is impossible for the wit of man to devise a narrative in which the wit of some other man cannot, and with some plausibility, find a hidden sense.

The field for self-deception, once we accept such methods of interpretation, is therefore obviously very wide. Yet in spite of this I think it impossible—for a reason I will give later—to abandon the method wholly when we are dealing, as Christians, with the Bible. We have, therefore, a steep hill before us. I will not attempt the cliffs. I must take a roundabout route which will look first as if it could never lead us to the top at all.

I begin far away from Scripture and even from Christianity, with instances of something said or written which takes on a new significance in the light of later events.

One of the Roman historians tells us about a fire in a provincial town which was thought to have originated in the public baths. What gave some colour to the suspicion of deliberate incendiarism was the fact that, earlier that day, a gentleman had complained that the water in the hot bath was only lukewarm and had received from an attendant the reply, *it will soon be hot enough*. Now of course if there really had been a plot, and the slave was in it, and fool enough to risk discovery by this veiled threat, then the story would not concern us. But let us suppose the fire was an accident (i.e. was intended by nobody). In that case the slave would have said something truer, or more importantly true, than he himself supposed. Clearly, there need be nothing here but chance coincidence. The slave's reply is fully explained by the customer's complaint; it is just what any bath attendant would say. The deeper significance which his words turned out to have during the next few hours was, as we should say, accidental.

Now let us take a somewhat tougher instance. (The non-classical reader needs to know that to a Roman the " age " or " reign " of Saturn meant the lost age of innocence and peace. That is, it roughly corresponded to the Garden of Eden before the Fall; though it was never, except among the Stoics, of anything like comparable importance.) Virgil, writing not very long before the birth of Christ, begins a poem thus : " The great procession of the ages begins anew. Now the Virgin returns, the reign of Saturn returns, and the new child is sent down from high heaven." It goes on to describe the paradisal age which this nativity will usher in. And of course throughout the Middle Ages it was taken that some dim pro-

phetic knowledge of the birth of Christ had reached
Virgil, probably through the Sibylline Books. He ranked
as a Pagan prophet. Modern scholars would, I suppose,
laugh at the idea. They might differ as to what noble or
imperial couple were being thus extravagantly compli-
mented by a court poet on the birth of a son; but the
resemblance to the birth of Christ would be regarded,
once more, as an accident. To say the least of it, however, this is a much more striking accident than the
slave's words to the man in the baths. If this is luck, it is
extraordinary luck. If one were a fanatical opponent of
Christianity one would be tempted to say, in an un-
guarded moment, that it was diabolically lucky.

I now turn to two examples which I think to be on a
different level. In them, as in those we have been considering, someone says what is truer and more important
than he knows; but it does not seem to me that he could
have done so by chance. I hasten to add that the alterna-
tive to chance which I have in mind is not "prophecy"
in the sense of clear prevision, miraculously bestowed.
Nor of course have I the slightest intention of using the
examples I shall cite as evidences for the truth of Christianity. Evidences are not here our subject. We are
merely considering how we should regard those second
meanings which things said or written sometimes take on
in the light of fuller knowledge than their author pos-
sessed. And I am suggesting that different instances
demand that we should regard them in different ways.
Sometimes we may regard this overtone as the result of
simple coincidence, however striking. But there are other
cases in which the later truth (which the speaker did not
know) is intimately related to the truth he did know;
so that, in hitting on something like it, he was in touch
with that very same reality in which the fuller truth is
rooted. Reading his words in the light of that fuller
truth and hearing it in them as an overtone or second
meaning, we are not foisting on them something alien
to his mind, an arbitrary addition. We are prolonging

his meaning in a direction congenial to it. The basic reality behind his words and behind the full truth is one and the same.

The status I claim for such things, then, is neither that of coincidence on the one hand nor that of supernatural prevision on the other. I will try to illustrate it by three imaginable cases. (i.) A holy person, explicitly claiming to prophesy by the Spirit, tells us that there is in the universe such and such a creature. Later we learn (which God forbid) to travel in space and distribute upon new worlds the vomit of our own corruption; and, sure enough, on the remote planet of some remote star, we find that very creature. This would be prophecy in the strictest sense. This would be evidence for the prophet's miraculous gift and strong presumptive evidence for the truth of anything else he had said. (ii.) A wholly unscientific writer of fantasies invents a creature for purely artistic reasons. Later on, we find a creature recognisably like it. This would be just the writer's luck. A man who knows nothing about racing may once in his life back a winner. (iii.) A great biologist, illustrating the relation between animal organisms and their environment, invents for this purpose a hypothetical animal adapted to a hypothetical environment. Later, we find a creature very like it (of course in an environment very like the one he had supposed). This resemblance is not in the least accidental. Insight and knowledge, not luck, led to his invention. The real nature of life explains both why there is such a creature in the universe and also why there was such a creature in his lectures. If, while we reread the lectures, we think of the reality, we are not bringing arbitrary fancies of our own to bear on the text. This second meaning is congenial to it. The examples I have in mind correspond to this third case; though, as we shall see, something more sensitive and personal than scientific knowledge is involved—what the writer or speaker was, not only what he knew.

Plato in his *Republic* is arguing that righteousness is

often praised for the rewards it brings—honour, popular-
ity, and the like—but that to see it in its true nature we
must separate it from all these, strip it naked. He asks
us therefore to imagine a perfectly righteous man treated
by all around him as a monster of wickedness. We must
picture him, still perfect, while he is bound, scourged, and
finally impaled (the Persian equivalent of crucifixion).
At this passage a Christian reader starts and rubs his
eyes. What is happening? Yet another of these lucky
coincidences? But presently he sees that there is something here which cannot be called luck at all.

Virgil, in the poem I have quoted, may have been, and
the slave in the baths almost certainly was, " talking
about something else ", some matter other than that of
which their words were most importantly true. Plato is
talking, and knows he is talking, about the fate of goodness in a wicked and misunderstanding world. But that
is not something simply other than the Passion of Christ.
It is the very same thing of which that Passion is the
supreme illustration. If Plato was in some measure
moved to write of it by the recent death—we may almost
say the martyrdom—of his master Socrates then that
again is not something simply other than the Passion of
Christ. The imperfect, yet very venerable, goodness of
Socrates led to the easy death of the hemlock, and the
perfect goodness of Christ led to the death of the cross,
not by chance but for the same reason; because goodness
is what it is, and because the fallen world is what it is. If
Plato, starting from one example and from his insight
into the nature of goodness and the nature of the world,
was led on to see the possibility of a perfect example, and
thus to depict something extremely like the Passion of
Christ, this happened not because he was lucky but because he was wise. If a man who knew only England and
had observed that, the higher a mountain was, the longer
it retained the snow in early spring, were led on to suppose a mountain so high that it retained the snow all the
year round, the similarity between his imagined moun-

tain and the real Alps would not be merely a lucky
accident. He might not know that there were any such
mountains in reality; just as Plato probably did not know
that the ideally perfect instance of crucified goodness
which he had depicted would ever become actual and
historical. But if that man ever saw the Alps he would
not say "What a curious coincidence". He would be
more likely to say "There! What did I tell you?"

And what are we to say of those gods in various Pagan
mythologies who are killed and rise again and who there-
by renew or transform the life of their worshippers or of
nature? The odd thing is that here those anthropologists
who are most hostile to our faith would agree with many
Christians in saying "The resemblance is not accidental". Of course the two parties would say this for different reasons. The anthropologists would mean: "All
these superstitions have a common source in the mind
and experience, especially the agricultural experience, of
early man. Your myth of Christ is like the myth of
Balder because it has the same origin. The likeness is a
family likeness." The Christians would fall into two
schools of thought. The early Fathers (or some of them),
who believed that Paganism was nothing but the direct
work of the Devil, would say: "The Devil has from the
beginning tried to mislead humanity with lies. As all
accomplished liars do, he makes his lies as like the truth
as he can; provided they lead man astray on the main
issue, the more closely they imitate truth the more effective they will be. That is why we call him God's Ape; he
is always imitating God. The resemblance of Adonis to
Christ is therefore not at all accidental; it is the resemblance we expect to find between a counterfeit and the
real thing, between a parody and the original, between
imitation pearls and pearls." Other Christians who
think, as I do, that in mythology divine and diabolical
and human elements (the desire for a good story), all
play a part, would say: "It is not accidental. In the
sequence of night and day, in the annual death and re-

birth of the crops, in the myths which these processes gave rise to, in the strong, if half-articulate, feeling (embodied in many Pagan " Mysteries ") that man himself must undergo some sort of death if he would truly live, there is already a likeness permitted by God to that truth on which all depends. The resemblance between these myths and the Christian truth is no more accidental than the resemblance between the sun and the sun's reflection in a pond, or that between a historical fact and the somewhat garbled version of it which lives in popular report, or between the trees and hills of the real world and the trees and hills in our dreams." Thus all three views alike would regard the " Pagan Christs " and the true Christ as things really related and would find the resemblance significant.

In other words, when we examine things said which take on, in the light of later knowledge, a meaning they could not have had for those who said them, they turn out to be of different sorts. To be sure, of whatever sort they may be, we can often profitably read them with that second meaning in mind. If I think (as I cannot help thinking) about the birth of Christ while I read that poem of Virgil's, or even if I make it a regular part of my Christmas reading, this may be quite a sensible and edifying thing to do. But the resemblance which makes such a reading possible may after all be a mere coincidence (though I am not sure that it is). I may be reading into Virgil what is wholly irrelevant to all he was, and did, and intended; irrelevant as the sinister meaning which the bathman's word in the Roman story acquired from later events may have been to anything that slave was or meant. But when I meditate on the Passion while reading Plato's picture of the Righteous One, or on the Resurrection while reading about Adonis or Balder, the case is altered. There is a real connection between what Plato and the myth-makers most deeply were and meant and what I believe to be the truth. I know that connection and they do not. But it is really there. It is not an arbitrary fancy of my own thrust upon the old words. One can, without any absurdity, imagine Plato or the myth-makers if they learned the truth, saying, " I see . . . so that was what I was really talking about. Of course. That is what my words really meant, and I never knew it." The bath attendant if innocent, on hearing the second meaning given to his words, would no doubt have said, " So help me, I never meant no such thing. Never come into my head. I hadn't a clue." What Virgil would have said, if he had learned the truth, I have no idea. (Or may we more charitably speak, not of what Plato and Virgil and the myth-makers " would have said " but of what they said? For we can pray with good hope that they now know and have long since welcomed the truth; " many shall come from the east and the west and sit down in the kingdom.")

Thus, long before we come to the Psalms or the Bible, there are good reasons for not throwing away all second meanings as rubbish. Keble said of the Pagan poets, " Thoughts beyond their thoughts to those high bards were given." But let us now turn to Scripture itself.

XI

SCRIPTURE

IF EVEN PAGAN utterances can carry a second meaning, not quite accidentally but because, in the sense I have suggested, they have a sort of right to it, we shall expect the Scriptures to do this more momentously and more often. We have two grounds for doing so if we are Christians.

i. For us these writings are " holy ", or " inspired ", or, as St. Paul says, " the Oracles of God ". But this has been understood in more than one way, and I must try to explain how I understand it, at least so far as the Old Testament is concerned. I have been suspected of being what is called a Fundamentalist. That is because I never regard any narrative as unhistorical simply on the ground that it includes the miraculous. Some people find the miraculous so hard to believe that they cannot imagine any reason for my acceptance of it other than a prior belief that every sentence of the Old Testament has historical or scientific truth. But this I do not hold, any more than St. Jerome did when he said that Moses described Creation " after the manner of a popular poet " (as we should say, mythically) or than Calvin did when he doubted whether the story of Job were history or fiction. The real reason why I can accept as historical a story in which a miracle occurs is that I have never found any philosophical grounds for the universal negative proposition that miracles do not happen. I have to decide on quite other grounds (if I decide at all) whether a given narrative is historical or not. The *Book of Job* appears to me unhistorical because it begins about a man quite unconnected with all history or even legend, with no genealogy, living in a country of which the Bible elsewhere has hardly anything to say; because, in fact, the author quite obviously writes as a story-teller not as a chronicler.

I have therefore no difficulty in accepting, say, the view of those scholars who tell us that the account of Creation in *Genesis* is derived from earlier Semitic stories which were Pagan and mythical. We must of course be quite clear what " derived from " means. Stories do not reproduce their species like mice. They are told by men. Each re-teller either repeats exactly what his predecessor had told him or else changes it. He may change it unknowingly or deliberately. If he changes it deliberately, his invention, his sense of form, his ethics, his ideas of what is fit, or edifying, or merely interesting, all come in. If unknowingly, then his unconscious (which is so largely responsible for our forgettings) has been at work. Thus at every step in what is called—a little misleadingly —the " evolution " of a story, a man, all he is and all his attitudes, are involved. And no good work is done anywhere without aid from the Father of Lights. When a series of such re-tellings turns a creation story which at first had almost no religious or metaphysical significance into a story which achieves the idea of true Creation and of a transcendent Creator (as *Genesis* does), then nothing will make me believe that some of the re-tellers, or some one of them, has not been guided by God.

Thus something originally merely natural—the kind of myth that is found amongst most nations—will have been raised by God above itself, qualified by Him and compelled by Him to serve purposes which of itself it would not have served. Generalising thus, I take it that the whole Old Testament consists of the same sort of material as any other literature—chronicle (some of it obviously pretty accurate), poems, moral and political diatribes, romances, and what not; but all taken into the service of God's word. Not all, I suppose, in the same way. There are prophets who write with the clearest awareness that Divine compulsion is upon them. There

are chroniclers whose intention may have been merely to
record. There are poets like those in the *Song of Songs*
who probably never dreamed of any but a secular and
natural purpose in what they composed. There is (and it
is no less important) the work first of the Jewish and then
of the Christian Church in preserving and canonising
just these books. There is the work of redactors and
editors in modifying them. On all of these I suppose a
Divine pressure; of which not by any means all need
have been conscious.

The human qualities of the raw materials show
through. Naïvety, error, contradiction, even (as in
the cursing Psalms) wickedness are not removed. The
total result is not " the Word of God " in the sense that
every passage, in itself, gives impeccable science or
history. It carries the Word of God; and we (under
grace, with attention to tradition and to interpreters
wiser than ourselves, and with the use of such intelligence
and learning as we may have) receive that word from it
not by using it as an encyclopædia or an encyclical but
by steeping ourselves in its tone or temper and so learning its over-all message.

To a human mind this working up (in a sense imper-
fectly), this sublimation (incomplete) of human
material, seems, no doubt, an untidy and leaky vehicle.
We might have expected, we may think we should have
preferred, an unrefracted light giving us ultimate truth
in systematic form—something we could have tabulated
and memorised and relied on like the multiplication
table. One can respect, and at moments envy, both the
Fundamentalist's view of the Bible and the Roman
Catholic's view of the Church. But there is one argument
which we should beware of using for either position :
God must have done what is best, this is best, therefore
God has done this. For we are mortals and do not know
what is best for us, and it is dangerous to prescribe what
God must have done—especially when we cannot, for the
life of us, see that He has after all done it.

We may observe that the teaching of Our Lord Himself, in which there is no imperfection, is not given us in that cut-and-dried, fool-proof, systematic fashion we might have expected or desired. He wrote no book. We have only reported sayings, most of them uttered in answer to questions, shaped in some degree by their context. And when we have collected them all we cannot reduce them to a system. He preaches but He does not lecture. He uses paradox, proverb, exaggeration, parable, irony; even (I mean no irreverence) the " wise-crack ". He utters maxims which, like popular proverbs, if rigorously taken, may seem to contradict one another. His teaching therefore cannot be grasped by the intellect alone, cannot be " got up " as if it were a " subject ". If we try to do that with it, we shall find Him the most elusive of teachers. He hardly ever gave a straight answer to a straight question. He will not be, in the way we want, " pinned down ". The attempt is (again, I mean no irreverence) like trying to bottle a sunbeam.

Descending lower, we find a somewhat similar difficulty with St. Paul. I cannot be the only reader who has wondered why God, having given him so many gifts, withheld from him (what would to us seem so necessary for the first Christian theologian) that of lucidity and orderly exposition.

Thus on three levels, in appropriate degrees, we meet the same refusal of what we might have thought best for us—in the Word Himself, in the Apostle of the Gentiles, in Scripture as a whole. Since this is what God has done, this, we must conclude, was best. It may be that what we should have liked would have been fatal to us if granted. It may be indispensable that our Lord's teaching, by that elusiveness (to our systematising intellect), should demand a response from the whole man, should make it so clear that there is no question of learning a subject but of steeping ourselves in a Personality, acquiring a new outlook and temper, breathing a new atmosphere, suffering Him, in His own way, to rebuild in us the defaced image of Himself. So in St. Paul. Perhaps the sort of works I should wish him to have written would have been useless. The crabbedness, the appearance of inconsequence and even of sophistry, the turbulent mixture of petty detail, personal complaint, practical advice, and lyrical rapture, finally let through what matters more than ideas—a whole Christian life in operation—better say, Christ Himself operating in a man's life. And in the same way, the value of the Old Testament may be dependent on what seems its imperfection. It may repel one use in order that we may be forced to use it in another way—to find the Word in it, not without repeated and leisurely reading nor without discriminations made by our conscience and our critical faculties, to re-live, while we read, the whole Jewish experience of God's gradual and graded self-revelation, to feel the very contentions between the Word and the human material through which it works. For here again, it is our total response that has to be elicited.

Certainly it seems to me that from having had to reach what is really the Voice of God in the cursing Psalms through all the horrible distortions of the human medium, I have gained something I might not have gained from a flawless, ethical exposition. The shadows have indicated (at least to my heart) something more about the light. Nor would I (now) willingly spare from my Bible something in itself so anti-religious as the nihilism of *Ecclesiastes*. We get there a clear, cold picture of man's life without God. That statement is itself part of God's word. We need to have heard it. Even to have assimilated *Ecclesiastes* and no other book in the Bible would be to have advanced further towards truth than some men do.

Admittedly these conjectures as to why God does what He does are probably of no more value than my dog's ideas of what I am up to when I sit and read. But though we can only guess the reasons, we can at least observe the consistency, of His ways. We read in *Genesis*

(2, 7) that God formed man of the dust and breathed life into him. For all the first writer knew of it, this passage might merely illustrate the survival, even in a truly creational story, of the Pagan inability to conceive true Creation, the savage, pictorial tendency to imagine God making things " out of " something as the potter or the carpenter does. Nevertheless, whether by lucky accident or (as I think) by God's guidance, it embodies a profound principle. For on any view man is in one sense clearly made " out of " something else. He is an animal; but an animal called to be, or raised to be, or (if you like) doomed to be, something more than an animal. On the ordinary biological view (what difficulties I have about evolution are not religious) one of the primates is changed so that he becomes man; but he remains still a primate and an animal. He is taken up into a new life without relinquishing the old. In the same way, all organic life takes up and uses processes merely chemical. But we can trace the principle higher as well as lower. For we are taught that the Incarnation itself proceeded " not by the conversion of the godhead into flesh, but by taking of (the) manhood into God "; in it human life becomes the vehicle of Divine life. If the Scriptures proceed not by conversion of God's word into a literature but by taking up of a literature to be a vehicle of God's word, this is not anomalous.

Of course, on almost all levels, that method seems to us precarious or, as I have said, leaky. None of these upgradings is, as we should have wished, self-evident. Because the lower nature, in being taken up and loaded with a new burden and advanced to a new privilege remains, and is not annihilated, it will always be possible to ignore the up-grading and see nothing but the lower. Thus men can read the life of Our Lord (because it is a human life) as nothing but a human life. Many, perhaps most, modern philosophies read human life merely as an animal life of unusual complexity. The Cartesians read animal life as mechanism. Just in the same way Scripture can be read as merely human literature. No new discovery, no new method, will ever give a final victory to either interpretation. For what is required, on all these levels alike, is not merely knowledge but a certain insight; getting the focus right. Those who can see in each of these instances only the lower will always be plausible. One who contended that a poem was nothing but black marks on white paper would be unanswerable if he addressed an audience who couldn't read. Look at it through microscopes, analyse the printer's ink and the paper, study it (in that way) as long as you like; you will never find something over and above all the products of analysis whereof you can say " This is the poem ". Those who can read, however, will continue to say the poem exists.

If the Old Testament is a literature thus " taken up ", made the vehicle of what is more than human, we can hardly set any limit to the weight or multiplicity of meanings which may have been laid upon it. If any writer may say more than he knows and mean more than he meant, then these writers will be especially likely to do so. And not by accident.

ii. The second reason for accepting the Old Testament in this way can be put more simply and is of course far more compulsive. We are committed to it in principle by Our Lord Himself. On that famous journey to Emmaus He found fault with the two disciples for not believing what the prophets had said. They ought to have known from their Bibles that the Anointed One, when He came, would enter his glory through suffering. He then explained, from " Moses " (i.e. the Pentateuch) down, all the places in the Old Testament " concerning Himself " (*Luke* 24, 25-27). He clearly identified Himself with a figure often mentioned in the Scriptures; appropriated to Himself many passages where a modern scholar might see no such reference. In the predictions of His Own Passion which He had previously made to the disciples, He was obviously doing the same thing. He accepted—indeed He claimed to be—the second meaning of Scripture.

We do not know—or anyway I do not know—what all these passages were. We can be pretty sure about one of them. The Ethiopian eunuch who met Philip (*Acts* 8, 27-38) was reading *Isaiah* 53. He did not know whether in that passage the prophet was talking about himself or about someone else. Philip, in answering the question, " preached unto him Jesus ". The answer, in fact, was " Isaiah is speaking of Jesus ". We need have no doubt that Philip's authority for this interpretation was Our Lord. (Our ancestors would have thought that Isaiah consciously foresaw the sufferings of Christ as people see the future in the sort of dreams recorded by Mr. Dunne. Modern scholars would say, that on the conscious level, he was referring to Israel itself, the whole nation personified. I do not see that it matters which view we take.) We can, again, be pretty sure, from the words on the cross (*Mark* 15, *34*), that Our Lord identified Himself with the sufferer in Psalm 22. Or when He asked (*Mark* 12, *35-36*) how Christ could be both David's son and David's lord, He clearly identified Christ, and therefore Himself, with the " my Lord " of Psalm 110— was in fact hinting at the mystery of the Incarnation by pointing out a difficulty which only it could solve. In *Matthew* 4, *6* the words of Psalm 91, *11, 12,* " He shall give his angels charge over thee . . . that thou hurt not thy foot against a stone," are applied to Him, and we may be sure the application was His own since only He could be the source of the temptation-story. In *Mark* 12, *10* He implicitly appropriates to Himself the words of Psalm 118, *22* about the stone which the builders rejected. " Thou shalt not leave my soul in hell, neither shalt thou suffer thy Holy One to see corruption " (16, *11*) is treated as a prophecy of His Resurrection in *Acts* 2, 27, and was doubtless so taken by Himself, since we find it so taken in the earliest Christian tradition—that is, by people likely to be closer both to the spirit and to the letter of

His words than any scholarship (I do not say, "any sanctity") will bring a modern. Yet it is, perhaps, idle to speak here of spirit and letter. There is almost no "letter" in the words of Jesus. Taken by a literalist, He will always prove the most elusive of teachers. Systems cannot keep up with that darting illumination. No net less wide than a man's whole heart, nor less fine of mesh than love, will hold the sacred Fish.

XII

SECOND MEANINGS IN THE PSALMS

IN A CERTAIN sense Our Lord's interpretation of the Psalms was common ground between Himself and His opponents. The question we mentioned a moment ago, how David can call Christ " my Lord " (*Mark* 12, 35-37), would lose its point unless it were addressed to those who took it for granted that the " my Lord " referred to in Psalm 110 was the Messiah, the regal and anointed deliverer who would subject the world to Israel. This method was accepted by all. The " scriptures " all had a " spiritual " or second sense. Even a gentile " God-fearer "[1] like the Ethiopian eunuch (*Acts* 8, 27-38) knew that the sacred books of Israel could not be understood without a guide, trained in the Judaic tradition, who could open the hidden meanings. Probably all instructed Jews in the first century saw references to the Messiah in most of those passages where Our Lord saw them; what was controversial was His identification of the Messianic King with another Old Testament figure and of both with Himself.

Two figures meet us in the Psalms, that of the sufferer and that of the conquering and liberating king. In 13, 22, 55 or 102, we have the Sufferer; in 2 or 72, the King. The Sufferer was, I think, by this time generally identified with (and may sometimes have originally been intended as) the whole nation, Israel itself—they would

---

[1] The " god-fearers " (*sebomenoi* or *metuentes*) were a recognised class of Gentiles who worshipped Jahveh without submitting to circumcision and the other ceremonial obligations of the Law. Cf. Psalm 118 (2, Jewish laity; 3 Jewish priests,; 4 God-fearers) and Acts 10, 2.

have said "himself". The King was the successor of David, the coming Messiah. Our Lord identified Himself with both these characters.

In principle, then, the allegorical way of reading the Psalms can claim the highest possible authority. But of course this does not mean that all the countless applications of it are fruitful, legitimate, or even rational. What we see when we think we are looking into the depths of Scripture may sometimes be only the reflection of our own silly faces. Many allegorical interpretations which were once popular seem to me, as perhaps to most moderns, to be strained, arbitrary and ridiculous. I think we may be sure that some of them really are; we ought to be much less sure that we know which. What seems strained—a mere triumph of perverse ingenuity—to one age, seems plain and obvious to another, so that our ancestors would often wonder how we could possibly miss what we wonder how they could have been silly-clever enough to find. And between different ages there is no impartial judge on earth, for no one stands outside the historical process; and of course no one is so completely enslaved to it as those who take our own age to be, not one more period, but a final and permanent platform from which we can see all other ages objectively.

Interpretations which were already established in the New Testament naturally have a special claim on our attention. We find in our Prayer Book that Psalm 110[1] is one of those appointed for Christmas Day. We may at first be surprised by this. There is nothing in it about peace and goodwill, nothing remotely suggestive of the stable at Bethlehem. It seems to have been originally either a coronation ode for a new king, promising conquest and empire, or a poem addressed to some king on the eve of a war, promising victory. It is full of threats. The "rod" of the king's power is to go forth from Jerusalem, foreign kings are to be wounded, battle fields to be covered with carnage, skulls cracked. The note is

[1] See Appendix I, p. 125.

not " Peace and goodwill " but " Beware. He's coming ".
Two things attach it to Christ with an authority far
beyond that of the Prayer Book. The first of course
(already mentioned) is that He Himself did so; He is the
" lord " whom " David " calls " my Lord ". The second
is the reference to Melchizedek (4). The identification
of this very mysterious person as a symbol or prophecy of
Christ is made in *Hebrews* 7. The exact form of the comment there made on *Genesis* 14 is no doubt alien to our
minds, but I think the essentials can all be retained in our
own idiom. We should certainly not argue from the
failure of *Genesis* to give Melchizedek any genealogy or
even parents that he has neither beginning nor end (if it
comes to that, Job has no genealogy either); but we
should be vividly aware that his unrelated, unaccounted
for, appearance sets him strangely apart from the texture
of the surrounding narrative. He comes from nowhere,
blesses in the name of the " most high God, possessor of
heaven and earth ", and utterly disappears. This gives
him the effect of belonging, if not to *the* Other World,
at any rate to *another* world; other than the story of
Abraham in general. He assumes without question, as the
writer of *Hebrews* saw, a superiority over Abraham
which Abraham accepts. He is an august, a " numin-
ous " figure. What the teller, or last re-teller, of *Genesis*
would have said if we asked him why he brought this
episode in or where he had got it from, I do not know.
I think, as I have explained, that a pressure from God
lay upon these tellings and re-tellings. And one effect
which the episode of Melchizedek was to have is quite
clear. It puts in, with unforgettable impressiveness, the
idea of a priesthood, not Pagan but a priesthood to the
one God, far earlier than the Jewish priesthood which
descends from Aaron, independent of the call to Abraham, somehow superior to Abraham's vocation. And this
older, pre-Judaic, priesthood is united with royalty;
Melchizedek is a priest-king. In some communities
priest-kings were normal, but not in Israel. It is thus

simply a fact that Melchizedek resembles (in his peculiar
way he is the only Old Testament character who resembles) Christ Himself. For He, like Melchizedek claims to
be Priest, though not of the priestly tribe, and also
King. Melchizedek really does point to Him; and so
of course does the hero of Psalm 110 who is a king but
also has the same sort of priesthood.

For a Jewish convert to Christianity this was extremely
important and removed a difficulty. He might be
brought to see how Christ was the successor of David;
it would be impossible to say that He was, in a similar
sense, the successor of Aaron. The idea of His priesthood
therefore involved the recognition of a priesthood independent of and superior to Aaron's. Melchizedek was
there to give this conception the sanction of the Scriptures. For us gentile Christians it is rather the other way
round. We are more likely to start from the priestly,
sacrificial, and intercessory character of Christ and
under-stress that of king and conqueror. Psalm 110, with
three other Christmas Psalms, corrects this. In 45 we
have again the almost threatening tone : " Gird thee with
thy sword upon thy thigh, O thou most mighty . . . thy
right hand shall teach thee terrible things . . . thy arrows
are very sharp " (4-6). In 89 we have the promises to
David (who would certainly mean all, or any, of David's
successors, just as " Jacob " can mean all his descendants). Foes are to fall before him (24). " David " will
call God " Father ", and God says " I will make him my
first-born " (27-28), that is " I will make him an eldes
son ", make him my heir, give him the whole world. In
132 we have "David" again; "As for his enemies,
shall clothe them with shame, but upon himself shall hi
crown flourish " (19). All this emphasises an aspect of th
Nativity to which our later sentiment about Christma
(excellent in itself) does less than justice. For those wh
first read these Psalms as poems about the birth of Chris
that birth primarily meant something very militant; th
hero, the " judge " or champion or giant-killer, who wa

to fight and beat death, hell and the devils, had at last
arrived, and the evidence suggests that Our Lord also
thought of Himself in those terms. (Milton's poem on
the *Nativity* well recaptures this side of Christmas.)

The assignment of Psalm 68[1] to Whitsunday has
some obvious reasons, even at a first reading. Verse *8,*
" The earth shook and the heavens dropped at the presence of God, even as Sinai also was moved," was, no
doubt, for the original writer a reference to the miracles
mentioned in *Exodus*, and thus foreshadows that very
different descent of God which came with the tongues of
fire. Verse *11* is a beautiful instance of the way in which
the old texts, almost inevitably charge themselves with
the new weight of meaning. The Prayer Book version
gives it as " The Lord gave the word, great was the
company of the preachers ". The " word " would be
the order for battle and its " preachers " (in rather a
grim sense) the triumphant Jewish warriors. But that
translation appears to be wrong. The verse really means
that there were many to spread " word " (i.e. the news) of
the victory. This will suit Pentecost quite as well. But I
think the real New Testament authority for assigning this
Psalm to Whitsunday appears in verse *18* (in the Prayer
Book, " Thou art gone up on high, thou hast led captivity captive, and received gifts for men "). According to
the scholars the Hebrew text here means that God, with
the armies of Israel as his agents, had taken huge masses
of prisoners and received " gifts " (booty or tribute) *from*
men. St. Paul, however (*Ephesians* 4, *8*) quotes a different reading : " When He ascended up on high He led
captivity captive and *gave* gifts *to* men." This must be
the passage which first associated the Psalm with the
coming of the Holy Ghost, for St. Paul is there speaking
of the gifts of the Spirit (*4-7*) and stressing the fact that
they come after the Ascension. After ascending, as a
result of ascending, Christ gives these gifts to men, or
receives these gifts (notice how the Prayer Book version

[1] See Appendix I, p. 120.

will now do well enough) from His Father " for men ", for the use of men, in order to transmit them to men. And this relation between the Ascension and the coming of the Spirit is of course in full accordance with Our Lord's own words, " It is expedient for you that I go away, for if I go not away the Comforter will not come unto you " (*John* 16, 7); as if the one were somehow impossible without the other, as if the Ascension, the withdrawal from the space-time in which our present senses operate, of the incarnate God, were the necessary condition of God's presence in another mode. There is a mystery here that I will not even attempt to sound.

That Psalm has led us through some complications; those in which Christ appears as the sufferer are very much easier. And it is here too that the second meaning is most inevitable. If Christ " tasted death for all men ", became the archetypal sufferer, then the expressions of all who ever suffered in the world are, from the very nature of things, related to His. Here (to speak in ludicrously human terms) we feel that it needed no Divine guidance to give the old texts their second meaning but would rather have needed a special miracle to keep it out. In Psalm 22, the terrible poem which Christ quoted in His final torture, it is not " they pierced my hands and my feet " (*17*), striking though this anticipation must always be, that really matters most. It is the union of total privation with total adherence to God, to a God who makes no response, simply because of what God is : " and thou continuest holy " (*3*). All the sufferings of the righteous speak here; but in 40, *15*, all the sufferings of the guilty too—" my sins have taken such hold upon me that I am not able to look up." But this too is for us the voice of Christ, for we have been taught that He who was without sin became sin for our sakes, plumbed the depth of that worst suffering which comes to evil men who at last know their own evil. Notice how this, in the original or literal sense, is hardly consistent with verses *8, 9,* and what counterpoint of truth this apparent contradiction takes on once the speaker is understood to be Christ.

But to say more of these suffering Psalms would be to labour the obvious. What I, at any rate, took longer to see was the full richness of that Christmas Psalm we have already mentioned, Psalm 45,[1] which shows us so many aspects of the Nativity we could never get from the carols or even (easily) from the gospels. This in its original intention was obviously a laureate ode on a royal wedding. (We are nowadays surprised to find that such an official bit of work, made " to order " by a court poet for a special occasion, should be good poetry. But in ages when the arts had their full health no one would have understood our surprise. All the great poets, painters, and musicians of old could produce great work " to order ". One who could not would have seemed as great a humbug as a captain who could navigate or a farmer who could farm only when the fit took him.) And simply as a marriage ode—what the Greeks call an *Epithalamium*— it is magnificent. But it is far more valuable for the light it throws on the Incarnation.

Few things once seemed to me more frigid and far-fetched than those interpretations, whether of this Psalm or of the *Song of Songs*, which identify the Bridegroom with Christ and the bride with the Church. Indeed, as we read the frank erotic poetry of the latter and contrast it with the edifying headlines in our Bibles, it is easy to be moved to a smile, even a cynically knowing smile, as if the pious interpreters were feigning an absurd innocence. I should still find it very hard to believe that anything like the " spiritual " sense was remotely intended by the original writers. But no one now (I fancy) who accepts that spiritual or second sense is denying, or saying anything against, the very plain sense which the writers did intend. The Psalm remains a rich, festive Epithalamium, the *Song* remains fine, sometimes exquisite, love poetry, and this is not in the

1 See Appendix I, p. 118.

least obliterated by the burden of the new meaning.
(Man is still one of the primates; a poem is still black
marks on white paper.) And later I began to see that the
new meaning is not arbitrary and springs from depths I
had not suspected. First, the language of nearly all great
mystics, not even in a common tradition, some of them
Pagan, some Islamic, most Christian, confronts us with
evidence that the image of marriage, of sexual union, is
not only profoundly natural but almost inevitable as a
means of expressing the desired union between God and
man. The very word " union " has already entailed some
such idea. Secondly, the god as bridegroom, his " holy
marriage " with the goddess, is a recurrent theme and a
recurrent ritual in many forms of Paganism—Paganism
not at what we should call its purest or most enlightened,
but perhaps at its most religious, at its most serious and
convinced. And if, as I believe, Christ, in transcending
and thus abrogating, also fulfils, both Paganism and
Judaism, then we may expect that He fulfils this side of
it too. This, as well as all else, is to be " summed up " in
Him. Thirdly, the idea appears, in a slightly different
form, within Judaism. For the mystics God is the Bridegroom of the individual soul. For the Pagans, the god is
the bridegroom of the mother-goddess, the earth, but his
union with her also makes fertile the whole tribe and its
livestock, so that in a sense he is their bridegroom too.
The Judaic conception is in some ways closer to the
Pagan than to that of the mystics, for in it the Bride of
God is the whole nation, Israel. This is worked out in
one of the most moving and graphic chapters of the
whole Old Testament (*Ezekiel* 16). Finally, this is transferred in the Apocalypse from the old Israel to the new,
and the Bride becomes the Church, " the whole blessed
company of faithful people ". It is this which has, like
the unworthy bride in Ezekiel, been rescued, washed,
clothed, and married by God—a marriage like King
Cophetua's. Thus the allegory which at first seemed
so arbitrary—the ingenuity of some prudish commenta-

tor who was determined to force flat edifications upon the most unpromising texts—turned out, when you seriously tugged at it, to have roots in the whole history of religion, to be loaded with poetry, to yield insights. To reject it because it does not immediately appeal to our own age is to be provincial, to have the self-complacent blindness of the stay-at-home.

Read in this sense, the Psalm restores Christmas to its proper complexity. The birth of Christ is the arrival of the great warrior and the great king. Also of the Lover, the Bridegroom, whose beauty surpasses that of man. But not only the Bridegroom as the lover, the desired; the Bridegroom also as he who makes fruitful, the father of children still to be begotten and born. (Certainly the image of a Child in a manger by no means suggests to us a king, giant-killer, bridegroom, and father. But it would not suggest the eternal Word either—if we didn't know. All alike are aspects of the same central paradox.) Then the poet turns to the Bride, with the exhortation, " forget also thine own people and thy father's house " (11). This sentence has a plain, and to us painful, sense while we read the Psalm as the poet probably intended it. One thinks of home-sickness, of a girl (probably a mere child) secretly crying in a strange *hareem*, of all the miseries which may underlie any dynastic marriage, especially an Oriental one. The poet (who of course knew all about this—he probably had a daughter of his own) consoles her : " Never mind, you have lost your parents but you will presently have children instead, and children who will be great men." But all this has also its poignant relevance when the Bride is the Church. A vocation is a terrible thing. To be called out of nature into the super-natural life is at first (or perhaps not quite at first—the wrench of the parting may be felt later) a costly honour. Even to be called from one natural level to another is loss as well as gain. Man has difficulties and sorrows which the other primates escape. But to be called up higher still costs still more. " Get thee out of thy country, and from

and from thy father's house ", said God to
enesis 12, *1*). It is a terrible command; turn
all you know. The consolation (if it will at
console) is very like that which the Psalmist
offers to the bride : " I will make of thee a great nation."
This " turn your back " is of course terribly repeated,
one may say aggravated, by Our Lord—" he that hateth
not father and mother and his own life." He speaks, as so
often, in the proverbial, paradoxical manner; hatred (in
cold prose) is not enjoined; only the resolute, the apparently ruthless, rejection of natural claims when, and
if, the terrible choice comes to that point. (Even so, this
text is, I take it, profitable only to those who read it with
horror. The man who finds it easy enough to hate his
father, the woman whose life is a long struggle not to
hate her mother, had probably best keep clear of it.) The
consolation of the Bride, in this allegory, consists, not
(where the mystics would put it) in the embraces of the
Spouse, but in her fruitfulness. If she does not bear fruit,
is not the mother of saints and sanctity, it may be supposed that the marriage was an illusion—for " a god's
embraces never are in vain ".

The choice of Psalm 8[1] for Ascension Day again depends on an interpretation found in the New Testament.
In its literal sense this short, exquisite lyric is simplicity
itself—an expression of wonder at man and man's place
in Nature (there is a chorus in Sophocles not unlike it)
and therefore at God who appointed it. God is wonderful both as champion or " judge " and as Creator. When
one looks up at the sky, and all the stars which are His
work, it seems strange that He should be concerned at all
with such things as man. Yet in fact, though He has
made us inferior to the celestial beings, He has, down
here on earth, given us extraordinary honour—made us
lords of all the other creatures. But to the writer of
Hebrews (*2, 6-9*) this suggested something which we, of
ourselves, would never have thought of. The Psalmist

[1] See Appendix I, p. 116.

said " Thou has put all things in subjection under his
(man's) feet " (6). The Christian writer observes that, in
the actual state of the universe, this is not strictly true.
Man is often killed, and still more often defeated, by
beasts, poisonous vegetables, weather, earthquakes, etc.
It would seem to us merely perverse and captious thus to
take a poetic expression as if it were intended for a
scientific universal. We can get nearest to the point of
view if we imagine the commentator arguing not (as I
think he actually does) " Since this is not true of the
present, and since all the scriptures must be true, the
statement must really refer to the future ", but rather,
" This is of course true in the poetic—and therefore, to a
logician, the loose—sense which the poet intended; but
how if it were far truer than he knew?" This will lead
us, by a route that is easier for our habits of mind, to
what he thinks the real meaning—or I should say the
" over-meaning ", the new weight laid upon the poet's
words. Christ has ascended into Heaven. And in due
time all things, quite strictly all, will be subjected to
Him. It is He who having been made (for a while)
" lower than the angels ", will become the conqueror and
ruler of all things, including death and (death's patron)
the devil.

To most of us this will seem a wire-drawn allegory.
But it is the very same which St. Paul obviously has in
mind in 1 *Corinthians* 15, *20-28*. This, with the passage
in *Hebrews*, makes it pretty certain that the interpretation was established in the earliest Christian tradition. It
may even descend from Our Lord. There was, after all,
no description of Himself which He delighted in more
than the " Son of Man "; and of course, just as " daughter of Babylon " means Babylon, so " Son of Man "
means Man, the Man, the archetypal Man, in whose
suffering, resurrection, and victories all men (unless they
refuse) can share.

And it is this, I believe, that most modern Christians
need to be reminded of. It seems to me that I seldom

meet any strong or exultant sense of the continued, never-to-be abandoned, Humanity of Christ in glory, in eternity. We stress the Humanity too exclusively at Christmas, and the Deity too exclusively after the Resurrection; almost as if Christ once became a man and then presently reverted to being simply a God. We think of the Resurrection and Ascension (rightly) as great acts of God; less often as the triumph of Man. The ancient interpretation of Psalm 8, however arrived at, is a cheering corrective. Nor, on further consideration, is the analogy of humanity's place in the universe (its greatness and littleness, its humble origins and—even on the natural level—amazing destiny) to the humiliation and victories of Christ, really strained and far-fetched. At least it does not seem so to me. As I have already indicated, there seems to me to be something more than analogy between the taking up of animality into man and the taking up of man into God.

But I walk in wonders beyond myself. It is time to conclude with a brief notice of some simpler things.

One is the apparent (and often no doubt real) self-righteousness of the Psalms: "Thou shalt find no wickedness in me" (17, 3), "I have walked innocently" (26, 1), "Preserve thou my soul, for I am holy" (86, 2). For many people it will not much mend matters if we say, as we probably can with truth, that sometimes the speaker was from the first intended to be Israel, not the individual; and even, within Israel, the faithful remnant. Yet it makes some difference; up to a certain point that remnant was holy and innocent compared with some of the surrounding Pagan cultures. It was often an "innocent sufferer" in the sense that it had not deserved what was inflicted on it, nor deserved it at the hands of those who inflicted it. But of course there was to come a Sufferer who was in fact holy and innocent. Plato's imaginary case was to become actual. All these assertions were to become true in His mouth. And if true, it was necessary they should be made. The lesson that perfect, unretaliating, forgiving innocence can lead, as the world is, not to love but to the screaming curses of the mob and to death, is essential. Our Lord therefore becomes the speaker in these passages when a Christian reads them; by right—it would be an obscuring of the real issue if He did not. For He denied all sin of Himself. (That, indeed, is no small argument of His Deity. For He has not often made even on the enemies of Christianity the impression of arrogance; many of them do not seem as shocked as we should expect at His claim to be "meek and lowly of heart". Yet He said such things as, on any hypothesis but one, would be the arrogance of a paranoiac. It is as if, even where the hypothesis is rejected, some of the reality which implies its truth "got across".)

Of the cursing Psalms I suppose most of us make our own moral allegories—well aware that these are personal and on a quite different level from the high matters I have been trying to handle. We know the proper object of utter hostility—wickedness, especially our own. Thus in 36, "My heart sheweth me the wickedness of the ungodly," each can reflect that his own heart is the specimen of that wickedness best known to him. After that, the upward plunge at verse 5 into the mercy high as heaven and the righteousness solid as the mountains takes on even more force and beauty. From this point of view I can use even the horrible passage in 137 about dashing the Babylonian babies against the stones. I know things in the inner world which are like babies; the infantile beginnings of small indulgences, small resentments, which may one day become dipsomania or settled hatred, but which woo us and wheedle us with special pleadings and seem so tiny, so helpless that in resisting them we feel we are being cruel to animals. They begin whimpering to us " I don't ask much, but ", or " I had at least hoped ", or " you owe yourself *some* consideration ". Against all such pretty infants (the dears have such winning ways)

the advice of the Psalm is the best. Knock the little
bastards' brains out. And "blessed" he who can, for it's
easier said than done.

Sometimes with no prompting from tradition a second
meaning will impose itself upon a reader irresistibly.
When the poet of Psalm 84 said (*10*) "For one day in
thy courts is better than a thousand", he doubtless
meant that one day there was better than a thousand
elsewhere. I find it impossible to exclude while I read
this the thought which, so far as I know, the Old Testament never quite reaches. It is there in the New, beauti-
fully introduced not by laying a new weight on old
words but more simply by adding to them. In Psalm 90
(*4*) it had been said that a thousand years were to God
like a single yesterday; in 2 *Peter* 3, *8*—not the first place
in the world where one would have looked for so metaphysical a theology—we read not only that a thousand
years are as one day but also that "one day is as a thousand years". The Psalmist only meant, I think, that God
was everlasting, that His life was infinite in time. But
the epistle takes us out of the time-series altogether. As
nothing outlasts God, so nothing slips away from Him
into a past. The later conception (later in Christian
thought—Plato had reached it) of the timeless as an
eternal present has been achieved. Ever afterwards,
for some of us, the "one day" in God's courts which is
better than a thousand, must carry a double meaning.
The Eternal may meet us in what is, by our present
measurements, a day, or (more likely) a minute or a
second; but we have touched what is not in any way
commensurable with lengths of time, whether long or
short. Hence our hope finally to emerge, if not altogether from time (that might not suit our humanity) at
any rate from the tyranny, the unilinear poverty, of
time, to ride it not to be ridden by it, and so to cure that
always aching wound (" the wound man was born for ")
which mere succession and mutability inflict on us,
almost equally when we are happy and when we are un-

happy. For we are so little reconciled to time that we are
even astonished at it. "How he's grown!" we exclaim,
"How time flies!" as though the universal form of our
experience were again and again a novelty. It is as
strange as if a fish were repeatedly surprised at the
wetness of water. And that would be strange indeed;
unless of course the fish were destined to become, one
day, a land animal.

APPENDIX I

SELECTED PSALMS

PSALM

8 *Domine, Dominus noster*

O Lord our Governor, how excellent is thy Name in all the world : thou that hast set thy glory above the heavens !

2. Out of the mouth of very babes and sucklings hast thou ordained strength, because of thine enemies : that thou mightest still the enemy and the avenger.

3. For I will consider thy heavens, even the works of thy fingers : the moon and the stars, which thou hast ordained.

4. What is man, that thou art mindful of him : and the son of man, that thou visitest him?

5. Thou madest him lower than the angels : to crown him with glory and worship.

6. Thou makest him to have dominion of the works of thy hands : and thou has put all things in subjection under his feet;

7. All sheep and oxen : yea, and the beasts of the field.

8. The fowls of the air, and the fishes of the sea : and whatsoever walketh through the paths of the seas.

9. O Lord our Governor : how excellent is thy Name in all the world !

19 *Coeli enarrant*

The heavens declare the glory of God : and the firmament sheweth his handywork

2. One day telleth another : and one night certifieth another.

PSALM

3. There is neither speech nor language: but their voices are heard among them.

4. Their sound is gone out into all lands: and their words into the ends of the world.

5. In them hath he set a tabernacle for the sun: which cometh forth as a bridegroom out of his chamber, and rejoiceth as a giant to run his course.

6. It goeth forth from the uttermost part of the heaven, and runneth about unto the end of it again: and there is nothing hid from the heat thereof.

7. The law of the Lord is an undefiled law, converting the soul: the testimony of the Lord is sure, and giveth wisdom unto the simple.

8. The statutes of the Lord are right, and rejoice the heart: the commandment of the Lord is pure, and giveth light unto the eyes.

9. The fear of the Lord is clean, and endureth for ever: the judgements of the Lord are true, and righteous altogether.

10. More to be desired are they than gold, yea, than much fine gold: sweeter also than honey, and the honeycomb.

11. Moreover, by them is thy servant taught: and in keeping of them there is great reward.

12. Who can tell how oft he offendeth: O cleanse thou me from my secret faults.

13. Keep thy servant also from presumptuous sins, lest they get the dominion over me: so shall I be undefiled, and innocent from the great offence.

14. Let the words of my mouth, and the meditation of my heart: be alway acceptable in thy sight.

15. O Lord: my strength, and my redeemer.

36 *Dixit injustus*

My heart sheweth me the wickedness of the ungodly: that there is no fear of God before his eyes.

PSALM

2. For he flattereth himself in his own sight : until his abominable sin be found out.

3. The words of his mouth are unrighteous, and full of deceit : he hath left off to behave himself wisely, and to do good.

4. He imagineth mischief upon his bed, and hath set himself in no good way : neither doth he abhor any thing that is evil.

5. Thy mercy, O Lord, reacheth unto the heavens : and thy faithfulness unto the clouds.

6. Thy righteousness standeth like the strong mountains : thy judgements are like the great deep.

7. Thou, Lord, shalt save both man and beast; How excellent is thy mercy, O God : and the children of men shall put their trust under the shadow of thy wings.

8. They shall be satisfied with the plenteousness of thy house : and thou shalt give them drink of thy pleasures, as out of the river.

9. For with thee is the well of life : and in thy light shall we see light.

10. O continue forth thy loving-kindness unto them that know thee : and thy righteousness unto them that are true of heart.

11. O let not the foot of pride come against me : and let not the hand of the ungodly cast me down.

12. There are they fallen, all that work wickedness : they are cast down, and shall not be able to stand.

45 *Eructavit cor meum*

My heart is inditing of a good matter : I speak of the things which I have made unto the King.

2. My tongue is the pen : of a ready writer.

3. Thou art fairer than the children of men : full of grace are thy lips, because God hath blessed thee for ever.

PSALM

4. Gird thee with thy sword upon thy thigh, O thou most Mighty : according to thy worship and renown.

5. Good luck have thou with thine honour : ride on, because of the word of truth, of meekness, and righteousness; and thy right hand shall teach thee terrible things.

6. The arrows are very sharp, and the people shall be subdued unto thee : even in the midst among the King's enemies.

7. Thy seat, O God, endureth for ever : the sceptre of thy kingdom is a right sceptre.

8. Thou hast loved righteousness, and hated iniquity : wherefore God, even thy God, hath anointed thee with the oil of gladness above thy fellows.

9. All the garments smell of myrrh, aloes, and cassia : out of the ivory palaces, whereby they have made thee glad.

10. King's daughters were among thy honourable women : upon thy right hand did stand the queen in a vesture of gold, wrought about with divers colours.

11. Hearken, O daughter, and consider, incline thine ear : forget also thine own people, and thy father's house.

12. So shall the King have pleasure in thy beauty : for he is thy Lord God, and worship thou him.

13. And the daughter of Tyre shall be there with a gift : like as the rich also among the people shall make their supplication before thee.

14. The King's daughter is all glorious within : her clothing is of wrought gold.

15. She shall be brought unto the King in raiment of needlework : the virgins that be her fellows shall bear her company, and shall be brought unto thee.

PSALM

16. With joy and gladness shall they be brought :
and shall enter into the King's palace.

17. Instead of thy fathers thou shalt have
children : whom thou mayest make princes in all
lands.

18. I will remember thy Name from one generation to another : therefore shall the people give
thanks unto thee, world without end.

68 *Exurgat Deus*

Let God arise,, and let his enemies be scattered :
let them also that hate him flee before him.

2. Like as the smoke vanisheth, so shalt thou
drive them away : and like as wax melteth at the
fire, so let the ungodly perish at the presence of
God.

3. But let the righteous be glad and rejoice before
God : let them also be merry and joyful.

4. O sing unto God, and sing praises unto his
Name : magnify him that rideth upon the heavens,
as it were upon an horse; praise him in his Name
JAH, and rejoice before him.

5. He is a Father of the fatherless, and defendeth
the cause of the widows : even God in his Holy
habitation.

6. He is the God that maketh men to be of one
mind in an house, and bringeth the prisoners out
of captivity : but letteth the runagates continue in
scarceness.

7. O God, when thou wentest forth before the
people : when thou wentest through the wilderness,

8. The earth shook, and the heavens dropped at
the presence of God : even as Sinai also was moved
at the presence of God, who is the God of Israel.

9. Thou, O God, sentest a gracious rain upon
thine inheritance : and refreshedst it when it was
weary.

PSALM

10. Thy congregation shall dwell therein: for thou, O God, hast of thy goodness prepared for the poor.

11. The Lord gave the word: great was the company of the preachers.

12. Kings with their armies did flee, and were discomfited: and they of the household divided the spoil.

13. Though ye have lien among the pots, yet shall ye be as the wings of a dove: that is covered with silver wings, and her feathers like gold.

14. When the Almighty scattered kings for their sake: then were they as white as snow in Salmon.

15. As the hill of Basan, so is God's hill: even an high hill, as the hill of Basan.

16. Why hop ye so, ye high hills? this is God's hill, in which it pleaseth him to dwell: yea, the Lord will abide in it for ever.

17. The chariots of God are twenty thousand, even thousands of angels: and the Lord is among them, as in the holy place of Sinai.

18. Thou art gone up on high, thou hast led captivity captive, and received gifts for men: yea, even from thine enemies, that the Lord God might dwell among them.

19. Praised be the Lord daily: even the God who helpeth us, and poureth his benefits upon us.

20. He is our God, even the God of whom cometh salvation: God is the Lord, by whom we escape death.

21. God shall wound the head of his enemies: and the hairy scalp of such a one as goeth on still in wickedness.

22. The Lord hath said, I will bring my people again, as I did from Basan: mine own will I bring again, as I did sometime from the deep of the sea.

23. That thy foot may be dipped in the blood of

thine enemies : and that the tongue of thy dogs may be red through the same.

24. It is well seen, O God, how thou goest : how thou, my God and King, goest in the sanctuary.

25. The singers go before, the minstrels follow after : in the midst are the damsels playing with the timbrels.

26. Give thanks, O Israel, unto God the Lord in the congregations : from the ground of the heart.

27. There is little Benjamin, their ruler, and the princes of Judah their counsel : the princes of Zebulon, and the princes of Nephthali.

28. Thy God hath sent forth strength for thee : stablish the thing, O God, that thou hast wrought in us.

29. For thy temple's sake at Jerusalem : so shall kings bring presents unto thee.

30. When the company of the spear-men, and multitude of the mighty are scattered abroad among the beasts of the people, so that they humbly bring pieces of silver : and when he hath scattered the people that delight in war;

31. Then shall the princes come out of Egypt : the Morians' land shall soon stretch out her hands unto God.

32. Sing unto God, O ye kingdoms of the earth : O sing praises unto the Lord.

33. Who sitteth in the heavens over all from the beginning : lo, he doth send out his voice, yea, and that a mighty voice.

34. Ascribe ye the power to God over Israel : his worship and strength is in the clouds.

35. O God, wonderful art thou in thy holy places : even the God of Israel; he will give strength and power unto his people; blessed be God.

PSALM

104 *Benedic, anima mea*

Praise the Lord, O my soul: O Lord my God thou art become exceeding glorious; thou art clothed with majesty and honour.

2. Thou deckest thyself with light as it were with a garment: and spreadest out the heavens like a curtain.

3. Who layeth the beams of his chambers in the waters: and maketh the clouds his chariot, and walketh upon the wings of the wind.

4. He maketh his angels spirits: and his ministers a flaming fire.

5. He laid the foundations of the earth: that it never should move at any time.

6. Thou coveredst it with the deep like as with a garment: the waters stand in the hills.

7. At thy rebuke they flee: at the voice of thy thunder they are afraid.

8. They go up as high as the hills, and down to the valleys beneath: even unto the place which thou hast appointed for them.

9. Thou hast set them their bounds which they shall not pass: neither turn again to cover the earth.

10. He sendeth the springs into the rivers: which run among the hills.

11. All beasts of the field drink thereof: and the wild asses quench their thirst.

12. Beside them shall the fowls of the air have their habitation: and sing among the branches.

13. He watereth the hills from above: the earth is filled with the fruit of thy works.

14. He bringeth forth grass for the cattle: and green herb for the service of men.

15. That he may bring food out of the earth, and wine that maketh glad the heart of man: and oil to

make him a cheerful countenance, and bread to strengthen man's heart.

16. The trees of the Lord also are full of sap: even the cedars of Libanus which he hath planted.

17. Wherein the birds make their nests: and the fir-trees are a dwelling for the stork.

18. The high hills are a refuge for the wild goats. and so are the stony rocks for the conies.

19. He appointed the moon for certain seasons: and the sun knoweth his going down.

20. Thou makest darkness that it may be night: wherein all the beasts of the forest do move.

21. The lions roaring after their prey: do seek their meat from God.

22. The sun ariseth, and they get them away together: and lay them down in their dens.

23. Man goeth forth to his work, and to his labour; until the evening.

24. O Lord, how manifold are thy works: in wisdom hast thou made them all; the earth is full of thy riches.

25. So is the great and wide sea also: wherein are things creeping innumerable, both small and great beasts.

26. There go the ships, and there is that Leviathan: whom thou hast made to take his pastime therein.

27. These wait all upon thee: that thou mayest give them their meat in due season.

28. When thou givest it them they gather it: and when thou openest thy hand they are filled with good.

29. When thou hidest thy face they are troubled: when thou takest away their breath they die, and are turned again to their dust.

30. When thou lettest thy breath go forth they

PSALM

shall be made : and thou shalt renew the face of the earth.

31. The glorious majesty of the Lord shall endure for ever : the Lord shall rejoice in his works.

32. The earth shall tremble at the look of him : if he do but touch the hills, they shall smoke.

33. I will sing unto the Lord as long as I live : I will praise my God while I have my being.

34. And so shall my words please him : my joy shall be in the Lord.

35. As for sinners, they shall be consumed out of the earth, and the ungodly shall come to an end : praise thou the Lord, O my soul, praise the Lord.

110 *Dixit Dominus*

The Lord said unto my Lord : Sit thou on my right hand, until I make thine enemies thy footstool.

2. The Lord shall send the rod of thy power out of Sion : be thou ruler, even in the midst among thine enemies.

3. In the day of thy power shall the people offer thee free-will offerings with an holy worship : the dew of thy birth is of the womb of the morning.

4. The Lord sware, and will not repent : Thou art a Priest for ever after the order of Melchisedech.

5. The Lord upon thy right hand : shall wound even kings in the day of his wrath.

6. He shall judge among the heathen; he shall fill the places with the dead bodies : and smite in sunder the heads over divers countries.

7. He shall drink of the brook in the way : therefore shall he lift up his head.

PSALMS DISCUSSED OR MENTIONED